# Practical Rust
# Web Projects

## Building Cloud and Web-Based
## Applications

Shing Lyu

Apress®

## *Practical Rust Web Projects: Building Cloud and Web-Based Applications*

Shing Lyu
Amsterdam, The Netherlands

ISBN-13 (pbk): 978-1-4842-6588-8     ISBN-13 (electronic): 978-1-4842-6589-5
https://doi.org/10.1007/978-1-4842-6589-5

Managing Director, Apress Media LLC: Welmoed Spahr
Acquisitions Editor: Steve Anglin
Development Editor: Matthew Moodie
Coordinating Editor: Mark Powers

Cover designed by eStudioCalamar

Cover image by Jason Leung on Unsplash (www.unsplash.com)

Distributed to the book trade worldwide by Apress Media, LLC, 1 New York Plaza, New York, NY 10004, U.S.A. Phone 1-800-SPRINGER, fax (201) 348-4505, e-mail orders-ny@springer-sbm.com, or visit www.springeronline.com. Apress Media, LLC is a California LLC and the sole member (owner) is Springer Science + Business Media Finance Inc (SSBM Finance Inc). SSBM Finance Inc is a **Delaware** corporation.

For information on translations, please e-mail booktranslations@springernature.com; for reprint, paperback, or audio rights, please e-mail bookpermissions@springernature.com.

Apress titles may be purchased in bulk for academic, corporate, or promotional use. eBook versions and licenses are also available for most titles. For more information, reference our Print and eBook Bulk Sales web page at http://www.apress.com/bulk-sales.

Any source code or other supplementary material referenced by the author in this book is available to readers on GitHub via the book's product page, located at www.apress.com/9781484265888. For more detailed information, please visit http://www.apress.com/source-code.

Printed on acid-free paper

*For my wife Wei-Chi, my father Ching-Chuan,*
*and my mother Man-Yun.*

# Table of Contents

# About the Author

 **Shing Lyu** is a software engineer who is passionate about open source software. He's worked with Rust professionally at Mozilla, on the Firefox (Gecko) and Servo browser engine project. Currently, he works at DAZN, a sports-streaming platform as a backend developer, with a focus on AWS and serverless technology. Shing has worked for many world-famous brands like Mozilla, Booking.com, and Intel. He is also active in the open source community. As one of the founders of the Taiwan Rust community, he loves to share his enthusiasm for Rust with others.

# About the Technical Reviewer

**Carlo Milanesi** is a professional software developer and expert in C++, graphics programming, and GUI design. He graduated from the State University of Milan and has worked in the financial and CAD/CAM software industries. He enjoys writing software in Smalltalk and Rust.

# CHAPTER 1

# Rust in the Web World

If you are reading this book, you are probably as excited about Rust as I am. Since the first stable release in 2015, Rust has come a long way in terms of features and stability. Developers around the world are fascinated about how Rust can combine features that were once thought of as unavoidable trade-offs: performance with memory safety, low-level control with productivity. Despite its infamous steep learning curve, Rust has gained popularity over the years. It was named the "most loved programming language" in a StackOverflow survey four years in a row, from 2016 to 2020. Many big companies and organizations—like Facebook, Microsoft, Dropbox, and npm—have started using Rust in production.

How are people using Rust? If we take a look at crates.io, the official Rust crates (libraries) registry, there are over 28,900 crates and over a billion downloads. There are 47 categories on crates.io,[1] ranging from the command-line interfaces, cryptography, databases, games, operating systems, and many more. But one of the most exciting fields is web programming. Many people spend most of their waking time online. There are roughly 1.5 billion websites on the World Wide Web. So it's natural that Rusticians are looking for ways to build websites and web applications with Rust.

---

[1]https://crates.io/categories

© Shing Lyu 2021
S. Lyu, *Practical Rust Web Projects*, https://doi.org/10.1007/978-1-4842-6589-5_1

---

**Note**    If you look for web development job postings nowadays, you'll come across the terms "frontend developer," "backend developer," and "full-stack developer." A frontend developer builds things that run in the *frontend*; usually, this is the end user's browser. A backend developer builds things that run in the *backend*, usually the server that acts as an HTTP server, WebSocket server, or other protocols. A full-stack developer works on both.

The typical technologies these roles need to work with include:

- Frontend: HTML, JavaScript, CSS, and WebAssembly (see Chapter 6).

- Backend: Web framework, REST API, database, WebSocket (see Chapters 2 to 5).

---

This book focuses on Rust for web applications. Since the backend is usually more language-agnostic, most of the chapters will be about the backend. We'll follow the history of how the backend evolves, starting with server-side-rendered websites. Then we'll develop REST APIs and WebSocket servers. Finally, we'll deploy this API onto the cloud using serverless technologies. That doesn't mean Rust can't be used in the frontend. With WebAssembly now available in most mainstream browsers, we can compile our Rust code to WebAssembly and run it in browsers. This unlocks a lot of potential for highly-performant applications in the frontend. After reading this book, you should have a good grasp of how to build a full-stack application in Rust.

# Who Is This Book For?

This book will be useful for:

- People who already know basic Rust syntax, but want to learn how to build web applications in Rust.

- People who are considering using Rust to build production-ready systems.

- People who have experience in web development and want to see how Rust can fit in.

If you already know how to code Rust, this book will help you learn web development in Rust. You have probably built a few command-line games and tools while reading *The Rust Book*[2] or other introductory courses. The final project in *The Rust Book* teaches you to build a toy web server. But how do you build production-ready web services? This book will introduce you to web frameworks and crates in order to apply your Rust skill on the web. If you already know web development in other languages (e.g., Node.js, Java, Go, Python, Ruby, etc.), this book will help you see how Rust makes it more secure and ergonomic to building web applications.

# Who Is This Book *Not* For?

This book might not be that useful for:

- People who want to learn the Rust programming language itself.

- People who want to learn the fundamentals of web development.

---

[2]https://doc.rust-lang.org/book/

This book is not a course on the Rust programming language itself, nor is it trying to teach Rust's syntax via examples. We'll focus on how to apply Rust to web applications, assuming you already know Rust's syntax and its language features. There are many excellent books on Rust, like *The Rust Programming Language* by Steve Klabnik and Carol Nichols. You can also find online books, interactive tutorials, and videos on the *Learn Rust* section of the official website.[3] I try to explain the fundamental web development concepts before implementing them. But this book does not focus on teaching general web development concepts through Rust, so the explanations will be brief. You'll get more out of this book if you already have some experience with web development in other languages.

# Criteria for Selecting Libraries

Rust is a relatively young language for web development. Therefore, although there are many frameworks and libraries out there, it was hard to decide which one to include in this book. The following sections cover the criteria for selecting which framework or library to use in this book.

## Pure-Rust

I try to find libraries that are built purely in Rust. Rust's FFI (foreign function interface) allows you to call existing C libraries (and many other languages) from Rust. Therefore, the easiest way to build Rust applications quickly is to leverage existing libraries in other languages. These libraries are usually designed with other languages in mind, so wrapping them in Rust results in a weird and not idiomatic Rust API. So if there are pure Rust libraries, I tend to choose those.

---

[3]https://www.rust-lang.org/learn

# Maturity

However, not every pure Rust library is mature. Because many Rust libraries are built from a clean slate, the developers tried to experiment with the latest technology, but that might mean that the architecture and API design is very fragile and changes frequently. Some of the libraries showed great potential in their early days, but then the development slowed down, and the projects eventually went into maintenance mode or were even abandoned. We aim to build useful software rather than experiment with exciting technologies and then throw the code away. Therefore, we need to be pragmatic and choose a library that is mature enough and uses widely-accepted design patterns.

# Popularity

If two or more candidates meet the previous criteria, I choose the most popular one. Popularity is based on a combination of factors, including:

- Number of downloads on crates.io

- Pace of development and release

- Discussions on issue trackers and discussion forums

- Media coverage

Although popularity is not a guarantee of success, a popular project is more likely to have a big enough community that supports it and keeps it alive. This can help us find a library that has the most potential to stick around longer in the future. You are also more likely to get support and answers online.

For backend-heavy chapters, I try to use plain JavaScript, HTML, and CSS, without additional frameworks like React.js, jQuery, or SCSS. This helps to keep the focus on the backend and avoid the need to learn a new framework that might be out of fashion soon.

# How To Use This Book

The chapters in this book do not strictly depend on each other. However, the example website in Chapters 2, 3, and 5 has the same functionality, but is built with different technologies. Reading these chapters in sequence will help you compare the pros and cons of each approach. Chapters 4 and 6 are relatively independent of the other chapters, so you can read them in any order.

# Chapter Overview

In Chapter 2, I started with the traditional form of website architecture: server-side rendered websites. You'll learn how to use the `actix-web` framework to set up a web server. Then, you'll learn how to render dynamic HTML pages using a template engine. To make the website even more interactive, you'll set up a database and render the website using the data in that database. Finally, you'll learn how to build a page that adds new information to the database.

In Chapter 3, you'll learn about a different website architecture that is popular among modern websites: using JavaScript to render dynamic data provided by a REST API. You'll learn how to return JSON-formatted data from the API. I also introduce other commonly used techniques that didn't fit into the previous chapter: input validation, error handling, logging, and enabling HTTPS.

In Chapter 4, you'll learn about a different protocol, WebSocket, that can help you build real-time, bidirectional communication. I'll show you how to use WebSocket to push real-time notifications to the client. Then you'll build a full-duplex chat application.

In Chapter 5, you'll learn how to build a REST API using AWS Lambda and other serverless services. You'll learn how to use the AWS SDK to communicate with the DynamoDB database. You'll also learn how to deploy the frontend to AWS S3 and connect it to the REST API. After finishing this chapter, you'll have a fully-functional website on the Internet without worrying about server maintenance.

In Chapter 6, I change the focus to the frontend. First, you'll learn how to compile your Rust code to WebAssembly (Wasm) so it can run in browsers. You'll build a JavaScript-Wasm hybrid image-processing application in the browser so you can leverage Wasm's high performance. Then you'll learn how to use a frontend framework to build the whole frontend application using only Rust.

# Source Code

All the source code for this book is available on GitHub at `https://github.com/apress/practical-rust-web-projects`. The source code is also accessible via the Download Source Code button located at `https://www.apress.com/us/book/9781484265888`.

When I include source code in the book, I only include the part that is relevant to the point being discussed. The irrelevant parts are omitted with comments like this:

```
// ...
```

Therefore, not all code examples can be compiled successfully. To check the fully working examples, use the source code on GitHub.

All the examples are developed and tested on a Linux (Ubuntu 16.04) machine. The Rust version is `stable-x86_64-unknown-linux-gnu unchanged - rustc 1.44.1 (c7087fe00 2020-06-17)`.

# CHAPTER 2

# Developing Websites

There is no denying that the web is one of the most popular platforms on Earth now. There are over 1.7 billion websites on the World Wide Web. And if you look at job boards for developers, web developers take up a large proportion of it. There are already many established programming languages for building the backend: Java, PHP, Python, Ruby, Node.js, and Go, just to name a few. But Rust fits perfectly into the web domain because of a few reasons:

- Security

- Concurrency

- Low-level control

Web security has been a big headache for everyone involved in building websites. But many vulnerabilities are due to bugs that can be caught by Rust's type checker and borrow checker. By having Rust check your code at compile-time, you can prevent many runtime vulnerabilities that might go undetected and be exploited when you least expect them to.

Nowadays, popular websites need to handle a large number of concurrent users. Therefore, concurrency and efficiency are crucial for web server software to handle more and more users. Rust's focus on "fearless concurrency" makes it easier to handle a large number of concurrent requests. The relatively new `async/await` syntax also makes async I/O more accessible to the average Rust programmer. On top of thread safety and async I/O, Rust's ability to control low-level CPU and memory opens up the possibility of squeezing more performance out of the server hardware.

© Shing Lyu 2021
S. Lyu, *Practical Rust Web Projects*, https://doi.org/10.1007/978-1-4842-6589-5_2

Rust also has a vibrant ecosystem that provides both high-level frameworks and low-level control over networking, database access, and type-safe templating. We are going to explore how to build a server-side rendered website in Rust.

# What Are You Building?

In the game Pokémon, there is a device called Pokédex, which is an index/ encyclopedia of all Pokémons. In this chapter, we are going to build a cat index called *Catdex*. The Catdex should have the following features:

- Show a list of cats. This demonstrates how to render a list of things using a server-side template.

- Read the cats from a database. This demonstrates how to set up a database with Object Relational Mapping (ORM).

- Use a form to add a new cat to the database. This demonstrates how to send POST requests and insert the data into a database.

- Show a specific detail page for each cat. This demonstrates how to read parameters from the URL path.

There are many ways to architect a website. One important distinction is server-side rendering versus client-side rendering. In server-side rendering, the HTML is generated on the server-side when a request comes in. In client-side rendering, the page is mostly generated in the browser by client-side frameworks like React, Vue, or Angular. The client-side framework then makes an HTTP request to a backend API to retrieve data that should go on the page. We'll talk about RESTful APIs in Chapter 3 and client-side rendering in Chapter 6. But in this chapter, we'll focus on server-side rendering.

We'll be using the `actix-web` framework as our web framework. `actix-web` doesn't dictate which template engine and database you should use. We'll be choosing the Handlebar for templating. For the database, we'll be using a PostgreSQL database through the Diesel ORM and `r2d2` connection pool.

# Hello World!

To start an Actix application, you first need to create an empty project with `cargo`, then add `actix-web` as dependencies. Run the following command in your terminal:

```
cargo new hello-world
cd hello-world
cargo install cargo-edit
cargo add actix-web
```

---

**Tip**  The `cargo-edit` extension will add a new command called `cargo add`. This helps you add new cargo dependencies without manually editing `Cargo.toml`.

---

Once `cargo` adds the dependencies, your `Cargo.toml` should look like Listing 2-1.

*Listing 2-1.* `Cargo.toml` for a Hello World Actix Application

**[package]**
```
name = "hello-world"
# ...
```

**[dependencies]**
```
actix-web = "3"
```

Now, open the src/main.rs file and copy Listing 2-2 into it.

***Listing 2-2.*** Hello World Actix Application

```
use actix_web::{web, App, HttpResponse, HttpServer, Responder};

async fn hello() -> impl Responder {
    HttpResponse::Ok().body("Hello world")
}

#[actix_web::main]
async fn main() -> std::io::Result<()> {
    println!("Listening on port 8080");
    HttpServer::new(|| {
        App::new().route("/hello", web::get().to(hello))
    })
    .bind("127.0.0.1:8080")?
    .run()
    .await
}
```

The core of Listing 2-2 is the App builder in the main() function. The App struct uses the builder pattern to build a new application instance. When you call route(), you specify which handler should be called when the user visits a specific path under the website. In this example, when the user visits /hello with an HTTP GET method (web::get()), it invokes the hello() handler.

The hello() handler is an async function that returns something that implements a Responder trait. A Responder is something that can be converted into an HTTP response. It's implemented on common types like &str, String, and u8 arrays. In this simple example, we respond with an HttpResponse::Ok() (i.e., status code 200) and a string body "Hello world".

An HttpServer wraps the App. The HttpServer handles the
incoming requests and passes them to the App. We bind() an address
(127.0.0.1:8080) to the server so it will listen on the specific IP and port.
Finally, we call run() to start the server and await on it. Notice that the
HttpServer doesn't take an App instance. Instead, it takes an App factory,
which is a simple closure that creates a new App instance every time. This is
because the HttpServer will create multiple worker threads, each running
one instance of the App. This way, we can better utilize multiple CPU cores
and achieve higher scalability.

You might also notice that the main() function is annotated with an
#[actix_web::main] attribute macro. This attribute tells Actix to execute
the main() function in a special runtime called actix-rt, which is built on
top of the popular Tokio[1] runtime.

---

**Note**    You might be aware that the functions in the "hello world"
program all have async in front, and you need to put .await
after them when calling. This is an important language feature
that makes it possible to build highly-efficient web servers. When
you call a normal (i.e., blocking) function, the whole thread blocks
and waits for the function to return. But if the function is async,
it immediately returns a Future instead of blocking. When you
.await on that Future, the program asynchronously waits for it
to complete, which allows other tasks on the same thread to make
progress.

---

[1]https://tokio.rs/

13

This is extremely important when building web servers. A modern web server usually needs to handle a large number of clients at the same time. If the server processes only one thing at a time and blocks whenever it's waiting for I/O (input/output) like in a socket communication, it can only serve one client at a time. One way to solve this is to use an operating system (OS) construct called a *process*. A process is an instance of your server program, and the OS allows you to start multiple processes. This way, you can have one process handling one client. But processes have a high overhead so this won't scale very well.

Another alternative is to use several threads. A thread is a series of instructions (and their surrounding execution context) that can run independently of other threads. Threads and processes are implemented differently in each operating system, but in general, a thread is a component of a process. Threads in the same process share some common resources like memory space, so they have a lower overhead to run than a process. Therefore, we can run more threads than processes on the same hardware, thus serving more clients.

However, because network I/O is much slower than CPU, most of the time, the threads are sitting idle, waiting for network I/O. Although threads are lighter than processes, they still have some overhead. By using async/await, we can potentially serve multiple clients per thread. When the server is waiting for a client's network I/O, it can yield the execution to other clients served by the same thread.

This is an overly simplified explanation of async/await and how it can help web development. If you want to learn more about the history and rationale of Rust's async/await design, watch Steve Klabnik's talk called "Rust's Journey to Async/Await."[2] You can also read the *Asynchronous Programming in Rust* book[3].

To run this example, simply run the `cargo run` command in the terminal under this project directory. A web server will start on `127.0.0.1:8080`, as we specified. Once the server is running, open a web browser and go to `http://127.0.0.1:8080/hello`, and you'll see the "Hello world" text (Figure 2-1).

*Figure 2-1.* Web server responding with "hello world"

## Serving Static Files

In the "hello world" example, we respond with a simple string. But most web pages are built with HTML (HyperText Markup Language). You could write HTML as a very long string in the Rust code and serve them that way, but it would be hard to manage. A more common way is to store the HTML as separate `.html` files and serve them with the web server. An HTML file usually also includes other CSS, JavaScript, or media files (e.g., images or videos). Actix allows you to serve all these files easily without explicitly writing code to read the file from disk.

---

[2]https://www.infoq.com/presentations/rust-2019/
[3]https://rust-lang.github.io/async-book/01_getting_started/01_chapter.html

First, let's create the files that will be served. Let's create a new project named catdex and add the dependencies. Then we'll create a folder called static, which will hold the static files. Under ./static/, we'll also create a css folder for CSS and an image folder for images:

```
cargo new catdex
cd catdex
cargo add actix-web actix-files
mkdir static
mkdir static/css
mkdir static/image
```

You can put some cat images (in JPEG format) in the static/image folder. We also need to create an index.css file in static/css that will be used by static/index.html.

```
.
+-- Cargo.lock
+-- Cargo.toml
+-- src
|    +-- main.rs
+-- static
     +-- css
     |    +-- index.css
     +-- image
     |    +-- british-short-hair.jpg
     |    +-- persian.jpg
     |    +-- ragdoll.jpg
     +-- index.html
```

Next, create a file called static/index.html and paste the HTML code in Listing 2-3 into it.

***Listing 2-3.*** A Minimal Static HTML

```html
<!DOCTYPE html>
<html>
  <head>
    <meta charset="UTF-8" />
    <title>Catdex</title>
  </head>
  <body>
    <h1>Catdex</h1>
  </body>
</html>
```

To serve this HTML file, you need to install the `actix-files` crate. We already did this in the previous `cargo add` step. Next, let's paste the following code into `src/main.rs` (Listing 2-4).

***Listing 2-4.*** Serving the `index.html` File

```rust
use actix_files::{NamedFile};
use actix_web::{web, App, HttpServer, Result};

async fn index() -> Result<NamedFile> {
    Ok(NamedFile::open("./static/index.html")?)
}

#[actix_web::main]
async fn main() -> std::io::Result<()> {
    println!("Listening on port 8080");
    HttpServer::new(|| {
        App::new()
            .route("/", web::get().to(index))
    })
```

17

```
.bind("127.0.0.1:8080")?
.run()
.await
```

The code is almost the same as the "hello world" example, except:

- The path is now / (root)

- The handler, named index(), now returns a NamedFile

The NamedFile::open() function opens the file in read-only mode. Because NamedFile implements Responder, we can return it directly in the handler. It's wrapped in a Result just in case the file reading failed.

If you run cargo run in a terminal, a server should start on port 8080. Then you can open a browser and go to http://127.0.0.1:8080/ and see the contents of index.html being rendered.

Since we are building a cat encyclopedia, we need to add some cat pictures. You can add the following HTML to static/index.html (Listing 2-5).

***Listing 2-5.*** index.html with External Image and CSS

```html
<!DOCTYPE html>
<html>
  <head>
    <meta charset="UTF-8" />
    <title>Catdex</title>
    <link rel="stylesheet" href="static/css/index.css"
     type="text/css">
  </head>
  <body>
    <h1>Catdex</h1>
    <section class="cats">
```

```
    <article class="cat">
      <h3>British short hair</h3>
      <img src="static/image/british-short-hair.jpg" />
    </article>
    <article class="cat">
      <h3>Persian</h3>
      <img src="static/image/persian.jpg" />
    </article>
    <article class="cat">
      <h3>Ragdoll</h3>
      <img src="static/image/ragdoll.jpg" />
    </article>
  </section>
 </body>
</html>
)
```

This file now imports four extra resources:

- `static/css/index.css`

- `static/image/british-short-hair.jpg`

- `static/image/persian.jpg`

- `static/image/ragdoll.jpg`

It's not scalable to write a custom path and handler for each individual resource. So instead, we need to tell Actix to serve every file under the `static` folder automatically. To achieve this, you can use the `actix-file::Files` service, which handles static files for you with some simple configuration. You need to register this service when you create the App. Add the code in Listing 2-6 to your `src/main.rs`.

***Listing 2-6.*** Using the Files Service to Serve Static Files

```rust
use actix_files::{Files, NamedFile};
use actix_web::{web, App, HttpServer, Result};

async fn index() -> Result<NamedFile> {
    Ok(NamedFile::open("./static/index.html")?)
}

#[actix_web::main]
async fn main() -> std::io::Result<()> {
    println!("Listening on port 8080");
    HttpServer::new(|| {
        App::new()
            .service(
                Files::new("/static", "static")
                    .show_files_listing(),
            )
            .route("/", web::get().to(index))
    })
    .bind("127.0.0.1:8080")?
    .run()
    .await
}
```

In the App factory, you can use the `.service()` function to attach a service to the application. The `Files` service will serve the static files in a folder (the second parameter, `static`) under a certain URL path (the first parameter, `/static`). You might notice that we also enabled `.show_files_listing()`. When this feature is turned on, you'll see an HTML list of all the files under the folder if you open the `/static` path (Figure 2-2). This is handy for debugging, but should be turned off in production to avoid security vulnerabilities[4].

---

[4]https://cwe.mitre.org/data/definitions/548.html

If you run `cargo run` and visit `http://localhost:8080/` in a browser, you'll see the Catdex now has images (Figure 2-3).

# Rendering Dynamic Templates

You might find that there is a pattern in Listing 2-5: each cat entry is an `<article>` containing a `<h3>` and an `<img>`. The only differences are the name and the image path. As you can imagine, when the number of cats goes up, this approach is not very salable. You end up writing many duplicated code. We can reuse the HTML structure by using a template. In a template, we define the HTML structure but fill in the image name and image path programmatically. Another side-benefit is that you can separate the presentation from the data. The HTML structure that defines how the page should look like is stored in the template, so you can focus on processing the data in Rust.

There are many template engines and syntax available. We choose Handlebars because of its popularity on crates.io. Handlebars was a JavaScript template engine, and it was ported to Rust. To install Handlebars, add the following crates to your `Cargo.toml` file (Listing 2-7).

**Index of /static**

- index.html
- image/
- css/

*Figure 2-2.* *File listing generated by* `.show_files_listing()`

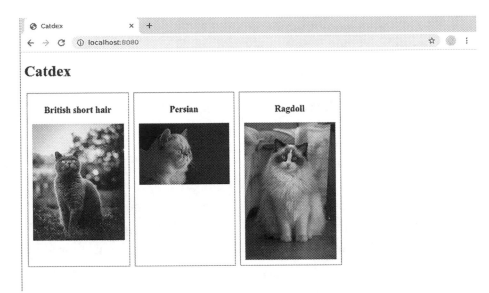

***Figure 2-3.*** *Catdex with hard-coded images*

***Listing 2-7.*** `Cargo.toml` for Handlebars

**[package]**
```
name = "catdex"

# ...
```

**[dependencies]**
```
# ...
serde_json = "1.0.53"
handlebars = { version = "3.0.1", features = ["dir_source"] }
```

Then you can turn the `static/index.html` file into a template, as shown in Listing 2-8.

**Listing 2-8.** Handlebars Template for Catdex

```html
<!DOCTYPE html>
<html>
  <head>
    <meta charset="UTF-8" />
    <title>{{project_name}}</title>
    <link rel="stylesheet" href="static/css/index.css"
     type="text/css">
  </head>
  <body>
    <h1>{{project_name}}</h1>
    <section class="cats">
      {{#each cats}}
        <article class="cat">
          <h3>{{this.name}}</h3>
          <img src="{{this.image_path}}" />
        </article>
      {{/each}}
    </section>
  </body>
</html>
```

The variables wrapped by {{}} are variables that we'll provide from the Rust code later. Notice that there is a {{#each}}...{{/each}} block. This #each block loops over an array and renders each element once using the template.

To use this template in the Actix code, you need to paste the code in Listing 2-9 into src/main.rs.

23

***Listing 2-9.***  Using Handlebars in Actix

```rust
use actix_files::Files;
use actix_web::{web, App, HttpResponse, HttpServer};

use handlebars::Handlebars;

async fn index(hb: web::Data<Handlebars<'_>>) -> HttpResponse {
    let data = json!({
        "project_name": "Catdex",
        "cats": [
            {
                "name": "British short hair",
                "image_path":
                    "/static/image/british-short-hair.jpg"
            },
            {
                "name": "Persian",
                "image_path": "/static/image/persian.jpg"
            },
            {
                "name": "Ragdoll",
                "image_path": "/static/image/ragdoll.jpg"
            }
        ]
    });

    let body = hb.render("index", &data).unwrap();

    HttpResponse::Ok().body(body)
}

#[actix_web::main]
async fn main() -> std::io::Result<()> {
    let mut handlebars = Handlebars::new();
```

```
handlebars
    .register_templates_directory(".html", "./static/")
    .unwrap();
let handlebars_ref = web::Data::new(handlebars);

println!("Listening on port 8080");
HttpServer::new(move || {
    App::new()
        .app_data(handlebars_ref.clone())
        .service(
            Files::new("/static", "static")
                .show_files_listing(),
        )
        .route("/", web::get().to(index))
})
.bind("127.0.0.1:8080")?
.run()
.await
}
```

Let's first focus on how the templates are loaded. Handlebars loads
and compiles the templates before using them. And it caches the compiled
templates so they don't need to be recompiled every time you use them.
Therefore, we can initialize the Handlebars template engine in the main()
function. To initialize a Handlebars instance, call Handlebars::new().
Then, we use the register_templates_directory() function to register
all the templates with the .html file extension in the ./static/ folder.
This function is guarded by a dir_source feature, which we enabled in
Cargo.toml (Listing 2-7).

As mentioned, Actix creates multiple App instances in multiple threads.
To avoid recompiling the templates in each thread, we need a way to
share this Handlebars instance across threads. To share states between
threads, you can use the web::Data provided by Actix. The shared state

wrapped inside `web::Data` must be shareable between threads. Luckily, Handlebars is `Send + Sync`, so it can be used in `web::Data`. We call the `web::Data::new()` function and pass the Handlebars instance to it.

The `web::Data` object is provided to the `App` builder by the `.app_data()` function. Because `web::Data` wraps this Handlebars with an `Arc` internally, we can cheaply clone it to give a copy to each `App` object. The `App` factory closure now needs to take ownership of the cloned `web::Data` object, so you need to add `move` for the closure.

The `index` handle gets the shared state from its parameter. You might notice that the parameter has the type `web::Data<Handlebars<' >>`. In the handler, you can use the `hb.render()` call to render the template. Remember that the template needs data to fill in the dynamic fields. The render function can take any data that implements the `Serialize` trait from the `serde`[5] crate. This means that anything that can be serialized is fine. For a quick demonstration, we use the `json!` macro so we can write some test data in JSON format. The `json!` macro will convert it into a `serde_json::Value`, which implements the `Serialize` trait.

As you can see in the code, the data we provide has two keys:

- `project_name`: A string that is used in the HTML `<title>` and `<h1>`.

- `cats`: An array of the cat's name and image path. This is used to generate the list of cats.

You can find that such keys are used in the template (Listing 2-8).

# Using a Database

So far, we hard-coded the data as a Rust variable. But that is useful only if we are building a static web page. If we want to create an interactive

---

[5] Quoting the official tagline: "Serde is a framework for serializing and deserializing Rust data structures efficiently and generically."

website where users can add, update, and remove cats, we need to store the data somewhere. One naïve way to implement this is to store them in a mut variable. But whenever the server restarts, the data is lost. The most common way to persists data is to use a database. It not only persists the data between server restarts, but it also provides more efficient query ability.

In this example, we are going to use PostgreSQL, a popular open source relational database. The database runs as a separate server, and our Actix application communicates with it over TCP/IP. In theory, we can write code that connects directly to the database with TCP/IP and issues raw SQL queries, but that would be too low-level for our use case. Instead, we are going to use an object-relational mapping (ORM) library to bridge between Rust code and database. An ORM allows you to manipulate data in the database as native Rust objects. The ORM will convert the Rust code to raw SQL under the hood and communicate with the database. It abstracts away the database so you can work with familiar Rust syntax. It also allows you to change the SQL engine (e.g., MySQL, SQLite) without rewriting all the code. The ORM we are going to use is called Diesel[6].

Before starting to use Diesel, you need to set up a PostgreSQL database. Most of the Linux distributions have it in their package repository, but they might not have the latest version. Also, the database usually starts automatically as a background daemon and consumes disk space, so installing it on an OS you use daily might be a little awkward. To make things simple, we choose to use a PostgreSQL installation, packaged as a Docker image. Docker is a container technology, which you can think of as a lightweight virtual machine. From the PostgreSQL server's perspective, the container provides an isolated OS where it can run. But it's lightweight because the container shares the host machine's OS kernel. This allows us to spin up a disposable Linux environment with PostgreSQL preinstalled. This will be easier to set up and clean up during development.

---

[6]https://diesel.rs/

First, you'll need to install Docker. Because this process varies drastically across Linux distributions, you'll need to find the instructions for your specific OS on `https://docs.docker.com/engine/install/`. For Debian-based Linux distributions, you can install it with `apt-get` after adding the repository[7].

After Docker is ready, you can start a Docker container containing a PostgreSQL server with the following command:

```
docker run \
  --name catdex-db \
  -e POSTGRES_PASSWORD=mypassword \
  -p 5432:5432 \
  -d \
  postgres:12.3-alpine
```

This simple line of code packs a lot of information:

- `postgres:12.3-alpine` is the name of the Docker image[8] used. This is an official image provided by Docker. The "alpine" in the name suggests it's built on top of Alpine Linux, a lightweight Linux distribution.

- `--name catdex-db` creates the Docker container with a custom name so we can identify it later.

- `-e POSTGRES_PASSWORD=mypassword` passes an environment variable into the container. In this case, the `POSTGRES_PASSWORD` variable will set the PostgreSQL's default password.

---

[7]`https://docs.docker.com/engine/install/debian/`
[8]`https://hub.docker.com/_/postgres`

- -p 5432:5432 maps the host machine's port 5432 to the container's port 5432. 5432 is the default port PostgreSQL uses.

- -d runs the container in detached mode, so it will run in the background without blocking the console.

You can verify that the container has been created and started by running docker ps.

Before we use Rust code to interact with the database, we can use the command-line client to test the database. Install the PostgreSQL command-line client psql with the following command[9]:

```
sudo apt-get install postgresql-client
```

Then you can connect to the database with the following:[10]

```
psql -h localhost -p 5432 --username=postgres --password=mypassword
```

You should be able to connect to the database and enter an interactive prompt. You can issue the \dt command to see the tables in the database (which should be empty at the moment). You can exit with either by using the \q command or by pressing Ctrl+D.

Once the database is up and running, we can start setting up Diesel. Diesel provides a command-line tool, which you can install using this command:

```
cargo install diesel_cli --no-default-features --features postgres
```

---

[9]The psql version you get from apt-get might not match your PostgreSQL server version. For most of the operations we are doing in this book, the version mismatch won't cause any problem. But if you are experiencing issues, try installing the psql client with the matching version from https://www.postgresql.org/download/.

[10]The username postgres is the default created by the postgres:12.3-alphine image.

Diesel can work with different databases, like MySQL and SQLite. By default, the CLI will work with all of them, but here we use the `--no-default-features` and `--features postgres` flags to tell cargo to only install the PostgreSQL integration. You might get a warning about the `ld` linker not being able to find the `pg` library. This is because, during the installation process, the tool needs to compile with the PostgreSQL headers. You can install the header files with:

```
sudo apt-get install libpq-dev
```

We need to tell the "`diesel`" command-line tool about the database's URL through an environment variable. Run this command in the terminal to set it:

```
export DATABASE_URL=postgres://postgres:mypassword@localhost
```

Then run the `diesel setup` command in the Catdex project directory. This will create a `migration` folder to keep the schema migration files, and a `diesel.toml` configuration file to tell the "`diesel`" tool to update the `src/schema.rs` file every time the schema updates.

Schema migration is a way to version-control your database schema. In the old days, database schema changes were made by database administrators (DBAs) or developers as ad hoc SQL commands. But without proper version control, you miss the ability to quickly roll back or rebuild the database from scratch. When using schema migration, you write a SQL script to apply the schema change (`up.sql`) and another script to revert the change (`down.sql`). By using such scripts, you should be able to change and revert your database schema easily. You can also bring an old database to the latest schema by applying all the migrations it missed. A migration tool will usually determine which migration needs to be applied, so you don't have to worry about it.

Let's create our first migration to set up our initial schema. Run this command to create a migration named `create_cats`:

```
diesel migration generate create_cats
```

30

This creates a folder in migrations/{yyyy-mm-dd-HHMMSS}_create_cats, with two files in it, named up.sql and down.sql.

In up.sql, let's write the SQL code to create the cats table (Listing 2-10).

***Listing 2-10.*** The up.sql File

```
CREATE TABLE cats (
  id SERIAL PRIMARY KEY,
  name VARCHAR NOT NULL,
  image_path VARCHAR NOT NULL
)
```

In down.sql, we need to write SQL that can undo what up.sql does (Listing 2-11).

***Listing 2-11.*** The down.sql File

```
DROP TABLE cats
```

Once the migration code is written, you can run diesel migration run to apply it. This should run the up.sql file.

---

**Tip**   The other two useful commands around migrations are:

- diesel migration revert: Runs the down.sql of the most recent migration.

- diesel migration redo: Runs the down.sql followed by up.sql of the most recent migration. After running these, your database should go back to the same state. This is useful for verifying that your down.sql works as intended.

---

If you connect to the database with psql again and issue the \dt command, you should be able to see the cats table.

Since we haven't implemented the page to add new cats, let's insert some test data using psql. Run this SQL command in psql:

```
INSERT INTO cats (name, image_path) VALUES
('Ragdoll', '/static/image/ragdoll.png');
```

Once we have some data in the database, we need to define the Rust struct that represents a row of the table. Create a new file called src/models.rs and paste the following code into it (Listing 2-12).

***Listing 2-12.*** Defining the ORM Model

```
use serde::{Deserialize, Serialize};
use super::schema::cats;

#[derive(Queryable, Serialize)]
pub struct Cat {
    pub id: i32,
    pub name: String,
    pub image_path: String
}
```

The fields of this model match the database schema. It also derives the Queryable trait so that we can use this type for SQL query results.

To use the module in the src/main.rs file, add the module import directive and the use directive to the beginning of the file:

```
mod models;
use self::models::*
```

It might be tempting to create a database connection inside the index() handler, right before we query the database. But the server will create a new connection whenever a new client makes a request. Establishing a connection to the database has a high overhead, so it would

be more efficient to keep a small pool of long-lived connections to the
database, so that every time an index() handler needs to make a database
query, it gets a free connection from the pool, then returns it to the pool
when it's done. This not only reduces the overhead of creating connections
but also reduces the stress on the database server because it has fewer
connections to manage. There is a connection pool implementation in
Rust called r2d2[11]. It works with Diesel using the diesel::r2d2 adapter
crate.

Another inefficiency regarding the database connection is that Diesel
only supports synchronous I/O. If we make a synchronous call to Diesel, the
thread that is running the request handler will be blocked. The thread pool
will soon be depleted and the server won't be able to serve more requests. To
mitigate this problem, we can use the actix_web::web::block() function.
This function takes a blocking function and executes it on a separate thread
pool, which is different from the Actix thread pool that executes request
handler. The web::block() function returns a future that's resolved when
the blocking database call finishes. This way, the request handler can yield
the execution to other handlers while it waits for the future to be resolved,
thus increasing the overall efficiency.

To add the r2d2 dependency to the project, you need to edit the
Cargo.toml file, as shown Listing 2-13.

***Listing 2-13.*** Add r2d2 to Cargo.toml

**[package]**
```
name = "catdex"
# ...
```

**[dependencies]**
```
actix-web = "3"
actix-files = "0.3.0"
```

---

[11]https://github.com/sfackler/r2d2

```
serde = "1.0.110"
serde_json = "1.0.53"
handlebars = { version = "3.0.1", features = ["dir_source"] }
diesel = { version = "1.4.4", features = ["postgres", "r2d2"] }
r2d2 = "0.8.8"
```

We not only add the r2d2 crate, but also enable the r2d2 feature on diesel. This in turn enables the diesel::r2d2 adapter.

Now, we need to set up the connection pool in our main function, before setting up the App. The modified main() function from Listing 2-9 is changed in Listing 2-14.

***Listing 2-14.*** Setting Up r2d2 Thread Pool

```
// ...
use actix_files::Files;
use actix_web::{
    http, web, App, Error, HttpResponse, HttpServer,
};

use handlebars::Handlebars;

use diesel::pg::PgConnection;
use diesel::prelude::*;
use diesel::r2d2::{self, ConnectionManager};

async fn index(hb: web::Data<Handlebars<'_>>) -> HttpResponse {
    // ...
}

#[actix_web::main]
async fn main() -> std::io::Result<()> {
    // Setting up the handlebar template engine
    let mut handlebars = Handlebars::new();
```

```
handlebars
    .register_templates_directory(".html", "./static/")
    .unwrap();

let handlebars_ref = web::Data::new(handlebars);

// Setting up the database connection pool
let database_url = env::var("DATABASE_URL")
    .expect("DATABASE_URL must be set");
let manager =
    ConnectionManager::<PgConnection>::new(&database_url);
let pool = r2d2::Pool::builder()
    .build(manager)
    .expect("Failed to create DB connection pool.");

println!("Listening on port 8080");
HttpServer::new(move || {
    App::new()
        .app_data(handlebars_ref.clone())
        .data(pool.clone())
        .service(
            Files::new("/static", "static")
                .show_files_listing(),
        )
        .route("/", web::get().to(index))
})
.bind("127.0.0.1:8080")?
.run()
.await
}
```

We first load the environment variable DATABASE_URL using env::var. This database URL is then passed to a ConnectionManager's new() function. The ConnectionManager implements the ManageConnection trait, which is how r2d2 keeps track of which connection is still active. This connection manager is passed to an r2d2::Pool::builder(), which builds the thread pool. The Pool created by r2d2::Pool::builder() is an Arc so it can be cloned and attached to the App using App::data.

---

**Note**    What's the difference between App::app_data and App::data?

Both App::app_data() and App::data() are for creating states in your Actix application. Because Actix creates a thread pool and runs one App instance per thread, you need to decide if the state needs to be shared across threads.

If you only want local states, which means each thread gets its own state and the states work independently from each other, you can use App::data().

If you want a global state that is shared across all threads, you need to construct a thread-safe pointer (usually an Arc) and clone() it to all threads. However, the App::data() function will wrap the state in an Arc internally, so it will result in an Arc wrapping another Arc. To avoid this double Arc, Actix allows you to construct a shared state with web::Data::new() and pass it using App::app_data(). App::app_data() won't wrap your shared state in an Arc.

There have been discussions[12] around clarifying or even simplifying the behavior of these two APIs, so this might change in the future.

---

The index handler no longer needs to create connections itself, but gets the connections from the pool (Listing 2-15).

---

[12]https://github.com/actix/actix-web/issues/1454

***Listing 2-15.*** Using the Connection Pool in the Index Handler

```rust
// ...
mod models;
mod schema;
use self::schema::cats::dsl::*; // provides alias like "cats"

// ...

async fn index(
    hb: web::Data<Handlebars<'_>>,
    pool: web::Data<DbPool>,
) -> Result<HttpResponse, Error> {

    let connection = pool.get()
        .expect("Can't get db connection from pool");

    let cats_data = web::block(move || {
        cats.limit(100).load::<Cat>(&connection)
    })
    .await
    .map_err(|_| HttpResponse::InternalServerError().finish())?;

    let data = IndexTemplateData {
        project_name: "Catdex".to_string(),
        cats: cats_data,
    };
    let body = hb.render("index", &data).unwrap();

    Ok(HttpResponse::Ok().body(body))
}
```

# Adding Cats with a Form

Now we can dynamically render the cats from the database, but there is no way to add new cats to the database from the page. We are going to build an HTML <form> that can perform an HTTP POST to the backend. The form will have two fields: the cat's name and an image. Create a new file called add.html in static (Listing 2-16).

*Listing 2-16.* The Add Cat Form

```html
<!DOCTYPE html>
<html>
  <head>
    <meta charset="UTF-8" />
    <title>Catdex</title>
    <link rel="stylesheet" href="static/css/index.css"
     type="text/css">
  </head>
  <body>
    <h1>Add a new cat</h1>

    <form action="add_cat_form" method="post"
     enctype="multipart/form-data">
      <label for="name">Name:</label>
      <input type="text" name="name" id="name" value="" />
      <label for="image">Image:</label>
      <input type="file" name="image" id="image" value="" />
      <button type="submit">Submit</button>
    </form>
  </body>
</html>
```

Notice that the `<form>` element has a few attributes that are very important:

- `method="post"`: This is the HTTP method used to submit the form. When using POST, the values are transmitted in the payload.

- `action="add_cat_form"`: The form will make a HTTP POST to `http://localhost:8080/add_cat_form`, which we'll handle later.

- `enctype="multipart/form-data"`: This controls the encoding of the POST body. The default is `application/x-www-form-urlencoded`, but it's better suited for small, textual data. Since we need to upload an image file, we choose to use the `multipart/form-data` encoding.

Although this page doesn't have any dynamic fields yet, let's still render it with Handlebars so we can easily make it dynamic if we need to. You can add a new handler called `add` and register it as a route in `App`, as shown in Listing 2-17.

***Listing 2-17.*** Adding the Add Route

```
async fn add(
    hb: web::Data<Handlebars<'_>>,
) -> Result<HttpResponse, Error> {
    let body = hb.render("add", &{}).unwrap();

    Ok(HttpResponse::Ok().body(body))
}

#[acitx_web::main]
async fn main() -> std::io::Result<()> {
    let mut handlebars = Handlebars::new();
    handlebars
```

```rust
        .register_templates_directory(".html", "./static/")
        .unwrap();

    let handlebars_ref = web::Data::new(handlebars);

    // ... setting up the database
    let pool = // ... creating the r2d2 pool

    println!("Listening on port 8080");
    HttpServer::new(move || {
        App::new()
            .app_data(handlebars_ref.clone())
            .data(pool.clone())
            .service(
                Files::new("/static", "static")
                    .show_files_listing(),
            )
            .route("/", web::get().to(index))
            .route("/add", web::get().to(add))
    })
    .bind("127.0.0.1:8080")?
    .run()
    .await
}
```

If you start the server again with cargo run, you can see this page by visiting http://localhost:8080/add (Figure 2-4).

Next, we need to build the /add cat form endpoint that receives the form's submission. As usual, we add an async function handler and register it in App. In the handler, we need to do a few things:

1.  Parse the request to get the cat name and the image file.

2.  Save the image file in the static folder.

3.  Get a database connection from the connection pool.

4.  Insert a new row into the database.

5.  Return a proper HTTP response.

Let's start by extracting the fields from the payload. To extract information from the request in a type-safe way, we can use *extractors*. The web::Data parameter we had in the index handler is an example of an extractor. Other extractors can get information from the path, the query parameters, the JSON payload, and the application/x-www-form-urlencoded form. The multipart payload extractor is available through the actix-multipart crate. However, the crate provides a low-level API, which is quite cumbersome to use. We'll use a higher-level crate that is built on actix-multipart, called awmp.

To add awmp, simply run cargo add awmp, or manually add awmp = "0.5.1" to your Cargo.toml. In the handler definition, add the awmp::Parts extractor as a parameter (Listing 2-18).

***Listing 2-18.*** Using the awmp::Parts Extractor

```
async fn add_cat_form(
    pool: web::Data<DbPool>,
    mut parts: Parts,
) -> Result<HttpResponse, Error> {
    let file_path = parts
        .files
        .take("image")
        .pop()
        .and_then(|f| f.persist_in("./static/image").ok())
        .unwrap_or_default();

    let text_fields: HashMap<_, _> =
        parts.texts.as_pairs().into_iter().collect();
```

```
    // TODO: Get a connection
    // TODO: Insert a row into the DB
    // TODO: Return a proper response
}
```

Because our form contains both textual and file fields, the Parts extractor puts them into files and texts, respectively. From files we can take() a field named image. It returns a Vec<File>. Because we know we have only one form field named image, we pop() the first File. Because pop() returns an Option, we use and_then() to get the file contained in it. Awmp stores this file as a temporary file using the tempfile crate, so we can call f.persist_in() to save it permanently into the ./static/image folder.

---

**Note**   In this example, we directly save the user-uploaded image into the static/image folder, which makes it available to be retrieved immediately. But in production, this violates many security best practices. For instance:

- An attacker might be able to upload a malicious executable or script file disguised as an image.

- An attacker can also use carefully crafted filenames to place files into a folder where they are not supposed to be.

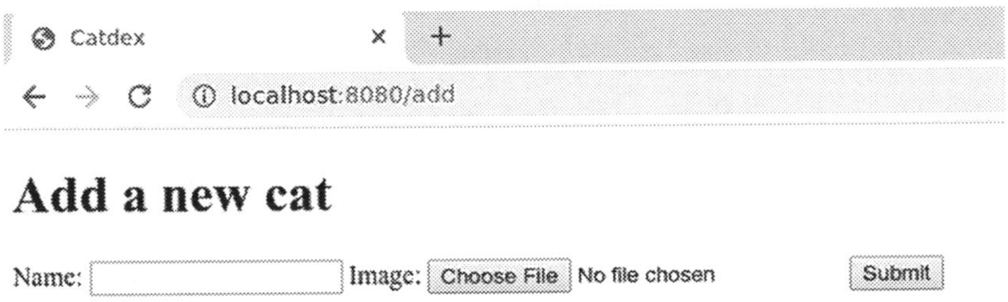

**Figure 2-4.**  *The add cat form*

- An attacker can also overwrite other people's images by uploading a file with the same name.

If you don't have enough security expertise, using a third-party file upload service is the easiest and most secure option. They usually provide some kind of SDK (Software Development Kit), so you can easily integrate them into your website. If you must build this in-house, there are a few ways you can secure the website:

- Only allow certain file extensions.

- Do not trust the file extension. Detect the file type to see if it matches the file extension.

- Scan the file with anti-virus software before saving it.

- Sanitize the filename.

- Randomize the filename.

You can find many more attack and defense strategies on the OWASP page titled "Unrestricted File Upload" at https://owasp.org/www-community/vulnerabilities/Unrestricted_File_Upload.

The texts fields contains all the text-based input fields in the form. It has an as_pairs() function that returns all the fields as a Vec of (key, value) tuples. We can easily convert it to a HashMap so we can get a particular key without scanning:

```
let text_fields: HashMap<_, _> =
    parts.texts.as_pairs().into_iter().collect();

// Example of getting a key's value:
text_fields.get("name").unwrap()
```

Now that we stored the file in the static/image folder and have all the text fields in a HashMap, we need to insert the row into the database. Since we are using an ORM, we need to construct a Cat struct and use diesel::insert_into().values(). But a problem quickly arises: The Cat struct we defined has three fields:

```
#[derive(Queryable, Serialize)]
pub struct Cat {
    pub id: i32,
    pub name: String,
    pub image_path: String
}
```

If we construct a Cat struct for insertion, we need to give it an id. But in our migration script, we declare the type of id to be SERIAL. PostgreSQL will auto-increment a SERIAL field whenever a new row is inserted. If we manually set ids, PostgreSQL will lose track of which id is used by the application, and this will generate conflicts. To let PostgreSQL generate the id, we need to define a new struct that omits the id field for insert. You can open the src/models.rs file and add a new struct, as shown in Listing 2-19.

***Listing 2-19.*** Model for Inserting Cats

```
#[derive(Insertable, Serialize, Deserialize)]
#[table_name = "cats"]
pub struct NewCat {
    // id will be added by the database
    pub name: String,
    pub image_path: String,
}
```

Not only is the id field omitted, the traits we defined are also a little different. Besides the Serialize trait and Deserialize trait that are required for serialization/deserialization, we also derive the `Insertable` trait. This tells `diesel` that it's a valid struct for inserting into the database. By default `diesel` assumes your struct name matches the table name. But since `Cats` is already taken, we can only name it `NewCat`. Therefore, we need to annotate it with `#[table_name = "cats"]` to specify which table it maps to.

Once we have this new struct, inserting the row into the database is as simple as Listing 2-20.

***Listing 2-20.*** Inserting a New Cat Into the Database

```
async fn add_cat_form(
    pool: web::Data<DbPool>,
    mut parts: Parts
) -> Result<HttpResponse, Error> {
    let file_path = // ...
    let text_fields: HashMap<_, _> = // ...

    let connection = pool.get()
        .expect("Can't get db connection from pool");

    let new_cat = NewCat {
        name: text_fields.get("name").unwrap().to_string(),
        image_path: file_path.to_string_lossy().to_string()
    };

    web::block(move ||
            diesel::insert_into(cats)
            .values(&new_cat)
            .execute(&connection)
        )
        .await
        .map_err(|_| {
```

```
            HttpResponse::InternalServerError().finish()
        }
    )?;
    // TODO: Return a proper response
}
```

Finally, we need to respond with a proper HTTP response. We can simply respond with a 201 Created status code indicating that the new resource (i.e., the cat) was created. But then the web page will remain in the same form. To improve the user experience, we can redirect the user back to the home page so they can see the new cat. This can be achieved by responding with a 303 See Other[13] status code with the Location header. When the browser receives this response, it will redirect the user to the URI specified in the Location header. So after putting everything together, the add_cat_form() handler should look like Listing 2-21.

***Listing 2-21.*** The Complete add_cat_form() Handler

```
async fn add_cat_form(
    pool: web::Data<DbPool>,
    mut parts: Parts
) -> Result<HttpResponse, Error> {
    let file_path = parts
        .files
        .take("image")
        .pop()
        .and_then(|f| f.persist("./static/image").ok())
        .unwrap_or_default();
    let text_fields: HashMap<_, _> =
        parts.texts.as_pairs().into_iter().collect();
```

---

[13]https://tools.ietf.org/html/rfc7231#section-6.4.4

```rust
let connection = pool.get()
    .expect("Can't get db connection from pool");

let new_cat = NewCat {
    name: text_fields.get("name").unwrap().to_string(),
    image_path: file_path.to_string_lossy().to_string(),
};

web::block(move || {
    diesel::insert_into(cats)
        .values(&new_cat)
        .execute(&connection)
})
.await
.map_err(|_| HttpResponse::InternalServerError().finish())?;

Ok(HttpResponse::SeeOther()
    .header(http::header::LOCATION, "/")
    .finish())
}
```

# Showing the Cat Detail Page

One last thing we missed is how to use parameters in the path. Since each cat in the database has an `id`, we can get a cat detail page using the following URL pattern: `/cat/<id>`. For example, `http://localhost:8080/cat/1` will show you a page about the cat with `id=1`.

Variables in the path can easily be extracted using the `web::Path` extractor. When we register the handler, we also need to specify which part of the path is a variable (Listing 2-22).

*Listing 2-22.* Extracting ID from the Path

```
// ...

async fn cat(
    hb: web::Data<Handlebars<'_>>,
    pool: web::Data<DbPool>,
    cat_id: web::Path<i32>,
) -> Result<HttpResponse, Error> {
    // TODO
}

#[actix_web::main]
async fn main() -> std::io::Result<()> {
    // ... Setting up handlebar and DB connection pool
    println!("Listening on port 8080");
    HttpServer::new(move || {
        App::new()
            .app_data(handlebars_ref.clone())
            .data(pool.clone())
            .service(
                Files::new("/static", "static")
                    .show_files_listing(),
            )
            .route("/", web::get().to(index))
            .route("/add", web::get().to(add))
            .route("/add_cat_form", web::post().to(add_cat_form))
            .route("/cat/{id}", web::get().to(cat))
            //                ^--- Variable
    })
    .bind("127.0.0.1:8080")?
    .run()
    .await
}
```

As you can see, when adding the route, we specify that the URL pattern is cat/{id}. In the cat() handler parameter, we specify that the cat_id: web::Path<i32> is a Path extractor that should extract the {id} as an integer.

We need to create a new handlebar template for this page, as shown in Listing 2-23.

***Listing 2-23.*** Cat Detail Page Template

```
<!DOCTYPE html>
<html>
  <head>
    <meta charset="UTF-8" />
    <title>{{name}}</title>
    <style type="text/css">
      img {
        max-width: 90vw;
        max-height: 80vh;
      }
    </style>
  </head>
  <body>
    <h1>{{name}}</h1>
    <img src="/{{image_path}}" />
    <p>
      <a href="/">Back</a>
    </p>
  </body>
</html>
```

The steps in the cat() handler are very straightforward:

1. Get a connection from the pool.

2. Query the database for the specific cat.

3. Render the page using Handlebars with data from the database.

This process is shown in Listing 2-24.

***Listing 2-24.*** The Cat Detail Page Handler

```
async fn cat(
    hb: web::Data<Handlebars<'_>>,
    pool: web::Data<DbPool>,
    cat_id: web::Path<i32>,
) -> Result<HttpResponse, Error> {
    let connection = pool.get()
        .expect("Can't get db connection from pool");

    let cat_data = web::block(move || {
        cats.filter(id.eq(cat_id.into_inner()))
            .first::<Cat>(&connection)
    })
    .await
    .map_err(|_| HttpResponse::InternalServerError().finish())?;

    let body = hb.render("cat", &cat_data).unwrap();

    Ok(HttpResponse::Ok().body(body))
}
```

The cat_id variable is a Path struct wrapping the actual i32 value, so we need to use cat_id.into_inner() to extract the integer ID. Then we do a filter query on the cats table to filter out only that cat with id == cat_id.

The `.filter()` function returns an array. Because we know that the ID is unique, we can safely take the first one with `.first()` and pass it to the template.

Now we have a working website that can:

- Add a cat with a form.

- Upload cat images.

- Show the list of cats from the database.

- Show a specific cat from the database.

There are many more details about building a website, like logging and error handling. But we'll leave that to the next chapter.

# Other Alternatives

There are many server-side frameworks in Rust to choose from. We are going to focus on high-level frameworks. Some people want to use low-level HTTP libraries like hyper[14] to build web servers for better control, but they require a better understanding of the underlying technology and more code.

If you are building a static website, you might not need a full-fledged dynamic web server framework. Instead, you can use a static site generator. Famous static site generators in Rust include Zola[15] and Cobalt[16].

---

[14]https://hyper.rs/

[15]https://www.getzola.org/

[16]https://cobalt-org.github.io/

If you need to build dynamic websites, there are many options besides actix-web. Rocket[17] is probably one of the strongest competitors. At the moment of writing, it has just switched from Nightly Rust to Stable, but hopefully it will stabilize soon. Warp[18] also gets a lot of attention in the community because of its unique design on composability, but the documentation and online resources are relatively scarce. There are a few others that are also relatively stable and easy to use:

- gotham[19]

- tower-web[20]

- iron[21]

- nickel[22]

- Tide[23]

- rouille[24]

- Thruster[25]

Some frameworks have their preference for a specific templating engine, and some keep it open (like actix-web). Besides Handlebars, there are many other template engines to choose from:

---

[17]https://rocket.rs/

[18]https://github.com/seanmonstar/warp

[19]https://gotham.rs/

[20]https://github.com/carllerche/tower-web

[21]http://github.com/iron/iron

[22]https://nickel-org.github.io/

[23]https://github.com/http-rs/tide

[24]https://github.com/tomaka/rouille

[25]https://github.com/thruster-rs/Thruster

- tera[26] (Jinja2/Django-inspired syntax)

- liquid[27]

- askama[28]

- tinytemplate[29]

- maud[30]

- ructe[31]

For database access through ORM, you can also check out Rustorm[32]. If you don't like using ORM and would like to work with raw SQL, you can find many client libraries for popular databases and in-memory cache:

- mysql[33] (for MySQL)

- postgres[34] (for PostgreSQL)

- mongodb[35] (for MongoDB)

- redis[36] (for Redis)

- memcache[37] (for Memcache)

You can find a complete list of web-related crates and get an overview of the maturity of Rust's web ecosystem at www.arewewebyet.org.

---

[26]https://tera.netlify.app/
[27]https://github.com/cobalt-org/liquid-rust
[28]https://github.com/djc/askama
[29]https://github.com/bheisler/TinyTemplate
[30]https://maud.lambda.xyz/
[31]https://github.com/kaj/ructe
[32]https://github.com/ivanceras/rustorm
[33]https://github.com/blackbeam/rust-mysql-simple
[34]https://github.com/sfackler/rust-postgres
[35]https://github.com/mongodb/mongo-rust-driver
[36]https://github.com/mitsuhiko/redis-rs
[37]https://github.com/aisk/rust-memcache

# CHAPTER 3

# REST APIs

In the previous chapter, we learned how to build a server-rendered website. However, there are a few drawbacks of using server-side rendering. First, whenever you navigate from one page to another or submit forms, the browser has to request a new page from the server. From the user's perspective, this means the browser will go blank for a second before the next page appears. With the rise of frontend frameworks like React, Angular, or Vue, this problem can be solved by rendering the page in the frontend with JavaScript. The frontend application makes requests to the server to get information or submit forms. The user can still interact with the page while it's requesting data, thanks to the asynchronous nature of JavaScript HTTP clients (e.g., built-in `fetch`). The server side now only needs to expose an HTTP RESTful API.[1]

A benefit of this architecture for the development team is that the backend and frontend team can work independently. They only need to negotiate an API contract and won't step on each other's toes. The frontend also doesn't need to be served by the application server anymore. Instead, it can be deployed in a separate server or managed service like AWS S3 and serve through a CDN for maximum performance.

But server-side rendering still has its strengths. For example, it works better with SEO (search engine optimization). Although nowadays many search engine's crawlers can partially understand JavaScript-rendered

---

[1]You can also use other protocols like SOAP, GraphQL, or gRPC, but we'll stick with REST in this chapter.

© Shing Lyu 2021
S. Lyu, *Practical Rust Web Projects*, https://doi.org/10.1007/978-1-4842-6589-5_3

pages, a server-side rendered page still works better. Another benefit is that the first page is interactive right away after it's loaded. For a client-side rendered page, the user will receive an empty page and need to wait for the API call to return with data.

In this chapter, we'll show you how to build REST APIs. We'll also discuss many backend topics that we didn't mention in the previous chapter, like input validation, error handling, logging, and testing.

# What Are You Building?

In this chapter, you are going to rebuild the Catdex as a REST API. You'll learn to build the following features:

- A RESTful API that returns the list of cats in JSON format.

- A frontend in HTML and JavaScript that consumes the API to display cats.

- Integration tests for the API endpoint.

- An API endpoint that returns a cat's detail in JSON, given that cat's ID.

- Input validation to check the ID is valid, and that returns a 400 Bad Request response.

- Custom error handling to prevent users from seeing unexpected errors from the server.

- Logging using the `Logging` middleware.

- Enabling HTTPS.

We'll still be using the `actix-web` framework to build the API. We'll not be using any frontend framework like React, but will write the page in vanilla JavaScript. This is because the focus of this chapter is not on the frontend. We'll touch upon how to write the frontend using a Rust framework in Chapter.6.

# Converting the Cats List to a REST API

Let's create a new `actix-web` project by running `cargo new catdex-api`.
In `Cargo.toml`, add `actix-web` and other dependencies you'll need in the
future (Listing 3-1).

*Listing 3-1.* `Cargo.toml`

**[package]**
```
name = "catdex-api"
version = "0.1.0"
edition = "2018"
```

**[dependencies]**
```
actix-web = "3"
actix-files = "0.3.0"
serde = "1.0.110"
serde_json = "1.0.53"
diesel = { version = "1.4.4", features = ["postgres", "r2d2"] }
r2d2 = "0.8.8"
```

In `src/main.rs`, first create a static server, as shown in Listing 3-2.

*Listing 3-2.* A Basic Static Server

```
use actix_files::Files;
use actix_web::{App, HttpServer};

#[actix_web::main]
async fn main() -> std::io::Result<()> {
    println!("Listening on port 8080");
    HttpServer::new(move || {
        App::new().service(
            Files::new("/", "static").show_files_listing(),
```

```
        )
    })
    .bind("127.0.0.1:8080")?
    .run()
    .await
}
```

**Tip**    We serve the static files in the `static` folder in the same server that will serve the REST APIs. This is just for ease of development. In production, you should consider serving the static resources (HTML, CSS, and JavaScript) from another server (e.g., Nginx) that's dedicated to serving static files. This gives you a few benefits:

- You can aggressively cache the static resources using a CDN (Content Delivery Network).

- Your static server and API server can scale independently.

- Deployment and maintenance might be easier.

We can also add the static files `static/index.html` (Listing 3-3) and `static/index.css` (Listing 3-4). Since there is no JavaScript in there yet, the page won't show any cats.

*Listing 3-3.* index.html

```html
<!DOCTYPE html>
<html>
  <head>
    <meta charset="UTF-8" />
    <title>Catdex</title>
```

```html
    <link rel="stylesheet" href="static/css/index.css"
     type="text/css">
  </head>
  <body>
    <h1>Catdex</h1>
    <p>
      <a href="/add.html">Add a new cat</a>
    </p>

    <section class="cats">
      <p>No cats yet</p>
    </section>
  </body>
</html>
```

***Listing 3-4.*** index.css

```css
.cats {
  display: flex;
}

.cat {
  border: 1px solid grey;
  min-width: 200px;
  min-height: 350px;
  margin: 5px;
  padding: 5px;
  text-align: center;
}

.cat > img {
  width: 190px;
}
```

In the previous chapter, the server responds with HTML rendered by
Handlebars. But for REST APIs, we need to return some structural data
so the frontend JavaScript can easily process it. JSON (JavaScript Object
Notation) is one of the most popular options. To construct a JSON response,
you can use `actix-web`'s `web::Json` helper to turn any serializable
(i.e., `impl serde::Serialize`) Rust object into an HTTP response. For
example, a minimal REST API endpoint that returns a hard-coded list of
cats can be implemented like in Listing 3-5. Notice that because `web::Json`
implements the `Responder` trait, you can simply return a `web::Json` from a
handler and `actix-web` will convert it to a proper HTTP response for you.

***Listing 3-5.*** A Minimal JSON API That Returns Hard-Coded Data

```rust
use actix_files::Files;
use actix_web::{http, web, App, Http, HttpServer, Responder};
use serde::Serialize;

#[derive(Serialize)]
pub struct Cat {
    pub id: i32,
    pub name: String,
    pub image_path: String,
}

async fn cats() -> impl Responder {
    let cats = vec![
        Cat {
            id: 1,
            name: "foo".to_string(),
            image_path: "foo.png".to_string(),
        },
        Cat {
            id: 2,
            name: "bar".to_string(),
```

```
            image_path: "bar.png".to_string(),
        },
    ];
    return web::Json(cats);
}

#[actix_web::main]
async fn main() -> std::io::Result<()> {
    println!("Listening on port 8080");
    HttpServer::new(move || {
        App::new()
            .service(
                web::scope("/api")
                    .route("/cats", web::get().to(cats)),
            )
            .service(
                Files::new("/", "static").show_files_listing(),
            )
    })
    .bind("127.0.0.1:8080")?
    .run()
    .await
}
```

Now you can run `cargo run` to start the server. You can test the API using curl[2]:

```
% curl localhost:8080/api/cats
[{"id":1,"name":"foo","image_path":"foo.png"},
{"id":2,"name":"bar","image_path":"bar.png"}]
```

---

[2]curl might not be installed in your distribution by default. For example, for Ubuntu you can install it with `sudo apt-get install curl`.

Of course, we are not satisfied with returning a static response. We
need to connect to a database. We can simply reuse the same PostgreSQL
database we created in the previous chapter. In the main() function, we
need to set up the r2d2 connection pool and Diesel connection similar to
what we've done before and copy the src/models.rs and src/schema.rs
from the Catdex project (Listing 3-6). Notice that the Cat struct definition
has been moved to src/model.rs.

***Listing 3-6.*** Setting Up the Database in main()

```
#[macro_use]
extern crate diesel;
// ...
use actix_web::{http, web, App, Http, Responder, HttpServer};
use diesel::pg::PgConnection;
use diesel::prelude::*;
use diesel::r2d2::{self, ConnectionManager};
use std::env;

mod models;
mod schema;
use self::models::*;
use self::schema::cats::dsl::*;
type DbPool = r2d2::Pool<ConnectionManager<PgConnection>>;

#[actix_web::main]
async fn main() -> std::io::Result<()> {
    let database_url = env::var("DATABASE_URL")
        .expect("DATABASE_URL must be set");
    let manager =
        ConnectionManager::<PgConnection>::new(&database_url);
    let pool = r2d2::Pool::builder()
        .build(manager)
        .expect("Failed to create DB connection pool.");
```

```
    println!("Listening on port 8080");
    HttpServer::new(move || {
        App::new()
            .data(pool.clone())
            .service(
                web::scope("/api").route(
                    "/cats",
                    web::get().to(cats_endpoint),
                ),
            )
            .service(
                Files::new("/", "static").show_files_listing(),
            )
    })
        .bind("127.0.0.1:8080")?
        .run()
        .await
}

// src/models.rs
use super::schema::cats;
use serde::{Deserialize, Serialize};

#[derive(Queryable, Serialize)]
pub struct Cat {
    pub id: i32,
    pub name: String,
    pub image_path: String,
}

// src/schema.rs
table! {
    cats (id) {
```

```
        id -> Int4,
        name -> Varchar,
        image_path -> Varchar,
    }
}
```

The cats API endpoint is also very similar to the previous index()
handler (Listing 3-7).

*Listing 3-7.* The Handler for /api/cats

```
async fn cats_endpoint(
    pool: web::Data<DbPool>,
) -> Result<HttpResponse, Error> {
    let connection = pool.get()
        .expect("Can't get db connection from pool");

    let cats_data = web::block(move || {
        cats.limit(100).load::<Cat>(&connection)
    })
    .await
    .map_err(|_| HttpResponse::InternalServerError().finish())?;
    return Ok(HttpResponse::Ok().json(cats_data));
}
```

The biggest difference is that we respond with an
HttpResponse::Ok().json(cats_data). Because cats_data is an
array of the Cats struct, and Cats implements serde::Serialize, the
.json() function can serialize it to a JSON string. We name the function
cats_endpoint instead of just cats because the name conflicts with the
table named cats defined by the Diesel schema.

If we restart the server and call it with curl again, we can see that the API returns cats from the database:

```
% curl localhost:8080/api/cats
[{"id":1,"name":"British short hair",
"image_path":"/static/image/british-short-hair.jpg"},
{"id":2,"name":"Persian","image_path":"/static/image/persian.jpg"},
{"id":3,"name":"Ragdoll","image_path":"/static/image/ragdoll.jpg"}]
```

If we format it for readability:

```
[
    {
        "id":1,
        "name":"British short hair",
        "image_path":"/static/image/british-short-hair.jpg"
    },
    {
        "id":2,
        "name":"Persian",
        "image_path":"/static/image/persian.jpg"
    },
    {
        "id":3,
        "name":"Ragdoll",
        "image_path":"/static/image/ragdoll.jpg"
    }
]
```

Now we can revisit our frontend page and make the page call the API
(Listing 3-8).[3]

*Listing 3-8.* Make the Frontend Call the API

```html
<!DOCTYPE html>
<html>
  <head>
    <meta charset="UTF-8" />
    <title>Catdex</title>
    <link rel="stylesheet" href="static/css/index.css"
     type="text/css">
  </head>
  <body>
    <h1>Catdex</h1>
    <p>
      <a href="/add.html">Add a new cat</a>
    </p>

    <section class="cats" id="cats">
      <p>No cats yet</p>
    </section>
    <script charset="utf-8">
      document.addEventListener("DOMContentLoaded", () => {
        fetch('/api/cats')
          .then((response) => response.json())
          .then((cats) => {
```

---

[3]You'll find a hack in this example. We remove the static prefix from the
image_path. This is because in the server we built for the previous chapter,
the images are served under the path /static/images/. But in this chapter's
example, we serve it under /images instead. To avoid having to re-create the
database and rebuild the add_cat form again, we just use this hack so we can look
at the important topics first.

```
            // Clear the "No cats yet"
            document.getElementById("cats").innerText = ""
            for (cat of cats) {
              const catElement = document.createElement("article")
              catElement.classList.add("cat")
              const catTitle = document.createElement("h3")
              const catLink = document.createElement("a")
              catLink.innerText = cat.name
              catLink.href = '/cat.html?id=${cat.id}'
              const catImage = document.createElement("img")
              // This is a hack to reuse the test data from
              // previous chapter
              catImage.src = cat.image_path
                  .replace(/\/static/, "")

              catTitle.appendChild(catLink)
              catElement.appendChild(catTitle)
              catElement.appendChild(catImage)

              document.getElementById("cats")
                .appendChild(catElement)
            }
          })
        })
    </script>
  </body>
</html>
```

We use the fetch() API to make the GET call and draw the cats we received onto the page with a series of document.createElement() and element.appendChild() calls. You can make this more declarative by adopting a frontend framework like React, but that is out of the scope of this chapter. This page now looks like Figure 3-1.

# API Testing

So far we've been testing our APIs manually. Automating this test process will not only help you reduce human labor, but also urges the developer to test more often and provide quick feedback. Rust comes with unit testing capability. You can unit test all your functions individually with it, and you can learn about it from the official Rust book.[4] In this book, instead, we'll be focusing on the integration test, in which you spin up a real HTTP server and test it with test requests.

actix-web provides a few helper functions to set up the test server and create test requests. A simple test that calls the /api/cats API should look like Listing 3-9.

***Listing 3-9.*** An Integration Test That Calls the /api/cats API

```
// ...
fn setup_database() -> DbPool {
    let database_url = env::var("DATABASE_URL")
        .expect("DATABASE_URL must be set");
    let manager =
        ConnectionManager::<PgConnection>::new(&database_url);
    r2d2::Pool::builder()
        .build(manager)
        .expect("Failed to create DB connection pool.")
}

#[actix_web::main]
async fn main() -> std::io::Result<()> {
    let pool = setup_database();
    // ...
}
```

---

[4]https://doc.rust-lang.org/book/ch11-00-testing.html

```rust
#[cfg(test)]
mod tests {
    use super::*;
    use actix_web::{test, App};

    #[actix_rt::test]
    async fn test_cats_endpoint_get() {
        let pool = setup_database();
        let mut app = test::init_service(
            App::new().data(pool.clone()).route(
                "/api/cats",
                web::get().to(cats_endpoint),
            ),
        )
        .await;
        let req = test::TestRequest::get()
            .uri("/api/cats")
            .to_request();
        let resp = test::call_service(&mut app, req).await;
        assert!(resp.status().is_success());
    }
}
```

## Catdex

Add a new cat

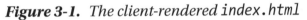

**Figure 3-1.** *The client-rendered* `index.html`

There are a few things to focus on in this example. First, we create a test module (`mod tests`) and add test cases as `async` functions. The test case functions need to be annotated with `#[actix_rt::test]`, so they will be run in the Actix runtime. Before running the test, you need to add the `actix_rt` crate using the `cargo add actix_rt` command.

Since we are doing an integration test, which involves starting a real HTTP server that communicates to a real database (as opposed to stubbing/mocking), we can reuse the code that sets up the database and connection pool by extracting it into a function named `setup_database`.

To start the test server, you construct an `App` instance as you would do in the `main()` function and pass it to `test::init_service()`. Of course, you can omit unrelated routes to make the code more readable and easier to debug. Then you can use the `test::TestRequest` builder to create a test request. Here we create a `GET` request for `/api/cats`. You can make the call with `test::call_service` and get the response. Finally, we can check if the response is a success (i.e., status code is in the 200-299 range) with an `assert!()`.

**Tip** For a test run to not interfere with any future test runs, you need to clean the database between every test run. You could create a test PostgreSQL database and use Rust code to set up and clean up before and after each test. But since we are using Docker and it's relatively easy to create new databases, you can consider creating a fresh PostgreSQL container for every test run and destroy it after the test finishes.

You might notice that the code that sets up the /api/cats route is duplicated in the main() function and in the test function. As your service gets more and more routes, this repetition will start making maintenance more difficult. actix-web provides a way to reuse configurations using the App::configure function. You pass a configuration function to App::new().configure(). The function needs to take one parameter of the type web::ServiceConfig. The ServiceConfig struct has the same interface as App, which has the methods data(), service(), route(), etc. We can create a function called api_config that sets up everything under the /api scope. This function can then be reused in the main() function and the integration test, as shown in Listing 3-10. The api_config() function can also be extracted into a separate module. So you can keep the configuration in a separate file to improve readability.

*Listing 3-10.* Reusing Configuration Using App::configure()

```
// ...

fn api_config(cfg: &mut web::ServiceConfig) {
    cfg.service(
        web::scope("/api")
            .route("/cats", web::get().to(cats_endpoint)),
    );
}
```

```
#[actix_web::main]
async fn main() -> std::io::Result<()> {
    let pool = setup_database();
    // ...
    HttpServer::new(move || {
        App::new()
            .data(pool.clone())
            .configure(api_config) // Used here
            .service(
                Files::new("/", "static").show_files_listing(),
            )
    })
    .bind("127.0.0.1:8080")?
    .run()
    .await
}

#[cfg(test)]
mod tests {
    use super::*;
    use actix_web::{test, App};

    #[actix_rt::test]
    async fn test_cats_endpoint_get() {
        let pool = setup_database();
        let mut app = test::init_service(
            App::new().data(pool.clone()).configure(api_config),
        )
        .await;
        let req = test::TestRequest::get()
            .uri("/api/cats")
            .to_request();
```

```
    let resp = test::call_service(&mut app, req).await;
    assert!(resp.status().is_success());
  }
}
```

# Building the Cat Detail API

The cats API is too simple for demonstrating advanced use cases like query parameter, input validation, and error handling, so we are going to rebuild the cat API so that it returns a single cat's detail.

First, let's take a look at how the frontend is supposed to call the API. You might have noticed that in Listing 3-8, each cat's name is a link that points to /cat.html?id=${cat.id}. This page doesn't exist yet, so you need to create it in static/cat.html and paste the code in Listing 3-11 into it.

*Listing 3-11.* Single Cat Detail Page

```
<!DOCTYPE html>
<html>
  <head>
    <meta charset="UTF-8" />
    <title>Cat</title>
    <link rel="stylesheet" href="/static/css/cat.css"
     type="text/css">
  </head>
  <body>
    <h1 id="name">Loading...</h1>
    <img id="image" />
    <p>
      <a href="/index.html">Back</a>
    </p>
```

```
<script charset="utf-8">
  const urlParams =
    new URLSearchParams(window.location.search)
  const cat_id = urlParams.get("id")
  document.addEventListener("DOMContentLoaded", () => {
    fetch('/api/cat/${cat_id}')
      .then((response) => response.json())
      .then((cat) => {
        document.getElementById("name").innerText = cat.name
        document.getElementById("image").src = cat.image_path
        document.title = cat.name
      })
  })
</script>
</body>
</html>
```

The link above opens the cat.html page and passes a query parameter
(e.g., ?id=1). This id query parameter is extracted as an object in JavaScript
by creating a new URLSearchParams(window.location.search) and then
calling the .get() function on it. With the cat's ID at hand, we can call the
/api/cat/${cat_id} API using fetch. The API has one path parameter
for the ID, and it should return the cat's detail (including the name and the
image path) in JSON format.

The most naïve implementation for this API would be like Listing 3-12.

*Listing 3-12.* A Naïve Implementation of the cat API

```
// ...

#[derive(Deserialize)]
struct CatEndpointPath {
    id: i32,
}
```

```
async fn cat_endpoint(
    pool: web::Data<DbPool>,
    cat_id: web::Path<CatEndpointPath>,
) -> Result<HttpResponse, Error> {
    let connection = pool.get()
        .expect("Can't get db connection from pool");

    let cat_data = web::block(move || {
        cats.filter(id.eq(cat_id.id)).first::<Cat>(&connection)
    })
    .await
    .map_err(|_| HttpResponse::InternalServerError().finish())?;

    Ok(HttpResponse::Ok().json(cat_data))
}

// ...

fn api_config(cfg: &mut web::ServiceConfig) {
    cfg.service(
        web::scope("/api")
            .route("/cats", web::get().to(cats_endpoint))
            .route("/cat/{id}", web::get().to(cat_endpoint)),
    );
}

#[actix_web::main]
async fn main() -> std::io::Result<()> {
    // ...
}
```

This code is very similar to the code we saw in the previous chapter. It extracts the cat_id using the web::Path<CatEndpointPath> extractor and tries to find it in the PostgreSQL database. But there are a few issues with this implementation:

- If it fails to get a connection from the connection pool, it will `panic!` due to the `expect` and will return a 500 error.

- If the ID does not exist in the database, we get a 500 `Internal Server Error`.

- If the ID in the path is not an integer (e.g., `/api/cat/abc`), it will return a 404 error with a message `cannot parse "abc" to an i16`.

- If the ID is an integer, but is not in the correct range (e.g., negative number), we get a 400 `Bad Request` error.

- It's not very obvious where and why the error occurs in the source code.

500 `Internal Server Error` is not very informative for the frontend. The frontend only knows that something went wrong on the server side, but it can't generate a helpful error message that will help the user work around the problem. There are a few ways to do it better:

- Return a 400[5] error when the ID is invalid (e.g., not a number, out of bounds).

- Return a 404 error when the ID doesn't exist in the database.

- Return a 500 error when we can't get a connection from the pool.

- Be able to customize the error message ourselves.

- Make it clear in the code where and why an error occurs.

---

[5]There are many debates about whether a 400 or a 422 is more appropriate in this case. We'll stick with the more generic 400 error.

# Input Validation

Let's deal with the input validation first. We know that the cat's ID can be wrong in many ways. If it's not an integer, actix-web's type-safe extractor will return a 404 error. This error can be customized, but we'll get back to it later. Let's first handle the case where the ID is an integer, but it's not in the sensible range.

Because our cat ID has the schema id SERIAL PRIMARY KEY, we know that PostgreSQL will start with 1 and increase by 1 every time we insert a new row. Therefore, the ID can't go below 1. Also, for the sake of the example, if we only allow a user to add unique cat breeds to the website, then there are only 71 standardized breeds recognized by The International Cat Association (TICA). If we keep some buffer and assume that the cat breeds might double in the future, we will have about $71 \times 2 = 142 \approx 150$ breeds. Therefore, we can check if the cat's ID is between 1 and 150 (inclusive); otherwise, we can simply reject the request without even querying the database.

To validate the input parameter in a more declarative way, you can use the validator and validator_derive crates. Add the crates with the command cargo add validator validator_derive. Let's apply that to the cat's ID, as shown in Listing 3-13.

***Listing 3-13.*** Using Validator On Cat's ID

```
use validator::Validate;
use validator_derive::Validate;

// ...

#[derive(Deserialize, Validate)]
struct CatEndpointPath {
    #[validate(range(min = 1, max = 150))]
    id: i32,
}
```

```
async fn cat_endpoint(
    pool: web::Data<DbPool>,
    cat_id: web::Path<CatEndpointPath>,
) -> Result<HttpResponse, Error> {
    cat_id
        .validate()
        .map_err(|_| HttpResponse::BadRequest().finish())?;

    // ... getting a connection and query from database
    Ok(HttpResponse::Ok().json(cat_data))
}
```

In this code snippet, the web::Path extractor now tries to extract the
CatEndpointPath struct from the URL. The CatEndpointPath is marked
to have a Validate auto-derive trait provided by the validator_derive
crate. This means you can call CatEndpointPath.validate() to validate
all its fields. Each field's validation rule can be annotated on it individually.
For our id we specify that it should be a number in the range of 1 to
150: #[validate(range(min=1, max=150))]. The validator crate also
provides some common checks like whether the field is an email, IP, URL,
or has a certain length.

Inside the cat_endpoint handler, we call cat_id.validate()
to validate. If the validation passes, it returns an Ok<()> and
we just allow the code to continue. If the validation fails, it
returns an Err<ValidationError>, and we convert it to an
HttpResponse::BadRequest and force it to return early with the ? operator.

If you start the server again with cargo run and make a call to the API
with an ID outside of the range (e.g., curl -v localhost:8080/api/cat/9999
or curl -v localhost:8080/api/cat/-1)[6], you should see the 400 Bad
Request response.

---

[6]The -v option is an abbreviation of --verbose. It will make curl print extra
information like the HTTP status code.

```
% curl -v localhost:8080/api/cat/9999
* Trying 127.0.0.1...
Connected to localhost (127.0.0.1) port 8080 (#0)
> GET /api/cat/9999 HTTP/1.1
> Host: localhost:8080
> User-Agent: curl/7.47.0
> Accept: */*
>
< HTTP/1.1 400 Bad Request
< content-length: 0
< date: Tue, 21 Jul 2020 10:05:21 GMT
<
Connection #0 to host localhost left intact
```

# Error Handling

You might notice that even this simple cat_endpoint handler can fail at many different points:

- The parameter validation might fail.

- Getting a connection from the connection pool might fail.

- Querying the cat from the database might fail because:

  - web::block() might fail for unexpected reasons.

  - Diesel ORM might fail for unexpected reasons.

  - The Diesel query might fail because the cat doesn't exist.[7]

---

[7]Although we make sure the ID is within 1 and 150, we might only have 70 cats in the database and someone might try to find a cat with ID 71.

Each of these errors might come from different libraries (`actix-web`, `r2d2`, `diesel`), and we've been converting them to HTTP response with `.map_err()` and `?`. But it's worth taking a step back and look at how `actix-web` handles errors.

Let's first look at what is an API endpoint handler's response: `Result<HttpResponse, Error>`. The `Error` here refers to `actix-web`'s own `actix_web::Error`[8], rather than the standard library `std::error::Error`. An `actix_web::Error` contains a trait object of the `ResponseError` trait. The `ResponseError` contains metadata (e.g., status code) and helper functions to construct an HTTP response, so `actix-web` can easily convert an `actix_web::Error` into an HTTP error response.

Since most of the errors returned by our dependent libraries are not `actix_web::Error`, if we have to handle them with `match` and construct an `actix_web::Error` by hand, the control flow will soon be very verbose. But in our previous example, we could do something like `.map_err(error::ErrorBadRequest)?;` or `.map_err(|_|HttpResponse::InternalServerError().finish())?;`. How did they work?

`actix-web` provides many helper functions and implicit type conversions to help you handle errors more fluently. But because there are so many ways, it can get confusing at times. So we'll break them down into four main categories:

- Using a `ResponseBuilder` object or a `Response` object.

- Using the `actix_web::error` helper functions like `actix_web::error::ErrorBadRequest`.

- Using a generic error that has implemented the `ResponseError` trait.

- Using a custom-built error type.

---

[8]It's actually a re-export of `actix_http::error::Error`. It's re-exported by `actix_ web` for convenience. `actix_web::error::Error` is the same thing.

# Using a ResponseBuilder or Response

The first way is the one we saw in Listing 3-13 and previous examples.
You'll often see this style of code in actix-web examples:

```
async fn cat_endpoint(
    pool: web::Data<DbPool>,
    cat_id: web::Path<CatEndpointPath>
) -> Result<HttpResponse, Error> {
    cat_id
        .validate()
        .map_err(|_| HttpResponse::BadRequest().finish())?;
    // ...
}
```

The validate() function returns a Result<(), ValidationErrors>.
We use the .map_err() function to convert the ValidationError
into an HttpResponse::BadRequest().finish(). You might be
surprised that we convert an error into a Response. At a first glance, we
are changing the return value into Result<HttpResponse, Response>.
But in fact, because the actix_web::error module implements
impl From<Response<Body>> for Error, a Response can be converted
to an Error with Error::from(response) (or response.into()). When
we use the ? operator to make the line return early in the case of Err,
the ? operator will implicitly use From to convert the Response into an
Error. So although we seem to return a response, it is converted to an
actix_web::Error.

There is also an implementation of impl From<ResponseBuilder> for Error. So even if you omit the finish() call, it will still work:

```
cat_id
    .validate()
    .map_err(|_| HttpResponse::BadRequest())?;
```

---

**Note**   If you are not familiar with the .map_err() function, its purpose is to convert the Err value of a Result from one type to another, leaving the Ok value unchanged. For example, if we pass a function that converts a value of type E to type F, the .map_err() will convert a Result<T, E> to Result<T, F>. This is useful for passing through the Ok value and handling the Err. In our example, we use it to convert the error to a type that actix-web accepts.

---

Figure 3-2 visualizes the error-handling flow we have so far using this method.

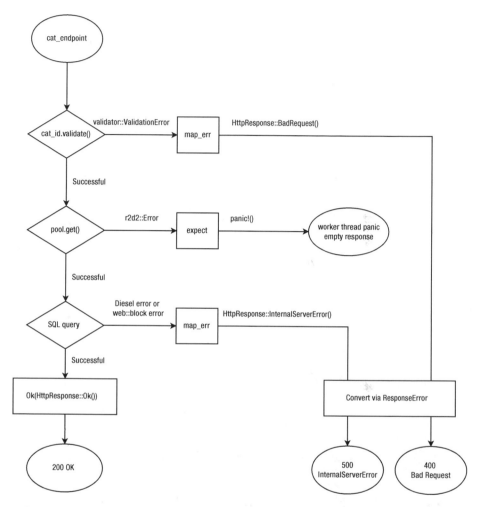

***Figure 3-2.*** *The current error-handling flow*

# Using the actix web::error Helpers

The first, and probably most straightforward, method is to use the
`actix_web::error` helpers. In the `actix_web::error` module, there are helper
functions for most of the commonly used HTTP status codes. For example:

- `ErrorBadRequest()`: 400

- `ErrorNotFound()`: 404

- `ErrorInternalServerError()`: 500

- `ErrorBadGateway()`: 502

These error helpers wrap any error and return an `actix_web::Error`. For example, the signature of `ErrorBadRequest` is as follows:

```
pub fn ErrorBadRequest<T>(err: T) -> Error
where
    T: Debug + Display + 'static,
```

Therefore, if we make a function call that may return a `Result<T, E>`, we can use the `.map_err()` function to convert the E into an `actix_web::Error`. Then, we can use the ? operator to force the handler function to return early with the converted `actix_web::Error`.

```
cat_id
    .validate()
    .map_err(|e| error::ErrorBadRequest(e))?;
```

Or simply replace the closure with the helper function:

```
cat_id
    .validate()
    .map_err(error::ErrorBadRequest)?;
```

# Using a Generic Error That Implemented the ResponseError Trait

The two previous methods convert (or wrap) the error we got into an `actix_web::Error`. But the type definition of `Responder` only requires the error to be `Into<Error>`. And since there is an implementation of `impl<T: ResponseError + 'static> From<T> for Error`, you can return anything that implements the `ResponseError` trait.

`actix-web` already implements `ResponseError` for many of the common error types you'll encounter in web services. For example,

- `std::io::error::Error`: When reading files.

- `serde_json::error::Error`: When serializing/deserializing JSON.

- `openssl::ssl::error::Error`: When making HTTPS connections.

Therefore, if you have some very simple handlers that have only one error, you can just return the error directly. For example, if we are serving the `index.html` by reading it in the handler with `NamedFile::open`, then we can simply return `std::io::Result<T>` (i.e., `Result<T, std::io::error::Error>`) and the `io::error::Error` can be converted to an HTTP response error without you writing anything extra (Listing 3-14).

***Listing 3-14.*** Returning an `io::Result`, Which Implements `ResponseError`

```
use actix_files::NamedFile;
use std::io;

fn index(_req: HttpRequest) -> io::Result<NamedFile> {
    Ok(NamedFile::open("static/index.html")?)
}
```

# Using a Custom-Built Error Type

The built-in implementations of `impl ResponseError for T` and `impl From<T> for Error` are helpful if you want to quickly return some error and don't want to deal with the conversion. But because many of the error types can be converted too easily, you might accidentally return some error that expose too much detail to the user. When building an API, you

need to carefully choose how much detail you expose to the user.
A very detailed error is useful for debugging, but it may expose too much
implementation detail and give attackers hints on hacking your system.
For example, if the application server fails to connect to the database, it
might be tempting to respond with an error describing why the database
connection failed, what the database IP and port are, or if you are really
not careful, what the database username and password are. This is all
useful information for an attacker to plan an attack based on the known
vulnerability of the kind of database you use. Instead, you should just
return a generic 500 Internal Server Error and don't let the client know
why. In other words, it's important to distinguish between the internal
error (e.g., database connection failed for a particular reason) and the
user-facing error (e.g., 500 Internal Server Error).

To achieve this separation, we can implement our custom error type
that implements the ResponseError trait. The error type can be an enum
with a detailed reason that helps debugging, but the ResponseError
implementation can convert these detailed errors into generic user-facing
errors. We can also customize the error message, instead of relying on the
default provided by the actix_web::error helpers or ResponseBuilder.

To define our custom error, let's create a new file called src/errors.rs
and create an enum called UserError, as shown in Listing 3-15.

***Listing 3-15.*** Custom Error Definition

```
#[derive(Debug)]
pub enum UserError {
    ValidationError,
    DBPoolGetError,
    NotFoundError,
    UnexpectedError,
}
```

Then let's declare this module in `src/main.rs` and use them in our cat endpoint (Listing 3-16).

***Listing 3-16.*** Declaring and Using the UserError in the `cat_endpoint`

```rust
// ...

mod errors;
use self::errors::UserError;

// ...

async fn cat_endpoint(
    pool: web::Data<DbPool>,
    cat_id: web::Path<CatEndpointPath>,
) -> Result<HttpResponse, UserError> {
    cat_id.validate().map_err(|_| UserError::ValidationError)?;
    let connection =
        pool.get().map_err(|_| UserError::DBPoolGetError)?;

    let query_id = cat_id.id.clone();
    let cat_data = web::block(move || {
        cats.filter(id.eq(query_id)).first::<Cat>(&connection)
    })
    .await
    .map_err(|e| match e {
        error::BlockingError::Error(
            diesel::result::Error::NotFound,
        ) => UserError::NotFoundError,
        _ => UserError::UnexpectedError,
    })?;
    Ok(HttpResponse::Ok().json(cat_data))
}
// ...
```

Notice that the cat_endpoint now returns the Result<HttpResponse, UserError> type. The .map_err() now converts the errors into UserError, instead of the error helper or ResponseBuilder. We also make a match in the .map_err() of the database query call, so we can isolate the special case where Diesel reports it can't find the cat (diesel::result::Error::NotFound).

The UserError has not implemented the ResponseError trait yet, so it can't be turned into an HTTP response. We can implement it in src/errors.rs, as shown in Listing 3-17. You'll also notice that we used the derive_more crate so we can auto-derive the Display trait on the UserError enum. You can add this crate by running cargo add derive_more.

***Listing 3-17.*** Implementing ResponseError for UserError

```
use actix_web::http::StatusCode;
use actix_web::{error, HttpResponse};
use derive_more::Display;
use serde_json::json;

#[derive(Display, Debug)]
pub enum UserError {
    #[display(fmt = "Invalid input parameter")]
    ValidationError,
    #[display(fmt = "Internal server error")]
    DBPoolGetError,
    #[display(fmt = "Not found")]
    NotFoundError,
    #[display(fmt = "Internal server error")]
    UnexpectedError,
}
```

```
impl error::ResponseError for UserError {
    fn error_response(&self) -> HttpResponse {
        HttpResponse::build(self.status_code())
            .json(json!({ "msg": self.to_string() }))
    }
    fn status_code(&self) -> StatusCode {
        match *self {
            UserError::ValidationError => {
                StatusCode::BAD_REQUEST
            }
            UserError::DBPoolGetError => {
                StatusCode::INTERNAL_SERVER_ERROR
            }
            UserError::NotFoundError => StatusCode::NOT_FOUND,
            UserError::UnexpectedError => {
                StatusCode::INTERNAL_SERVER_ERROR
            }
        }
    }
}
```

An HTTP response has two key elements: the status code and the body. The status code is determined by the status_code() function. The function is a simple match that converts the enum variant to the appropriate status code. For the body, we want to respond with a JSON of the format:

```
{
    "msg": "An error message"
}
```

The HTTP response is generated in the error_response() function using the HttpResponse builder. The message body is created by calling self.to_string(). We derive the Display trait on the enum and annotate each variant with `#[display(fmt="...")]`, so that the `.to_string()` function will convert the enum variant to the string we specified. The JSON body is serialized using the `json!()` macro from `serde_json`.

With this custom error, we can create as many internal errors as we want, and then convert them to something general for the user. Also because the return type is `Result<HttpResponse,UserError>`, type check will prevent you from accidentally returning an error that happens to implement `ResponseError`.

Figure 3-3 visualizes the new error-handling flow after using `UserError`.

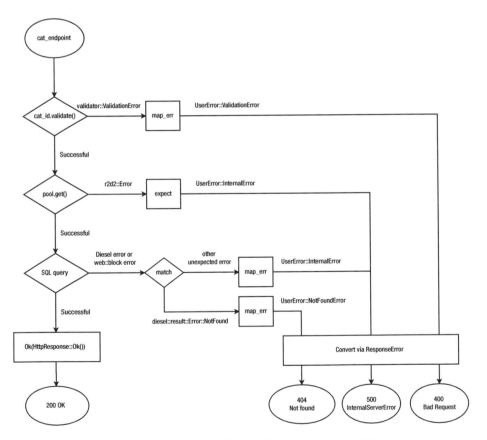

**Figure 3-3.** *The error-handling flow after using* `UserError`

# Customize the web::Path Extractor Error

We now have control over most of the errors, but we missed one case. If the ID cannot be converted to i32, the web::Path extractor will return a 404 Not Found with a default error message. But that error can also be customized through web::PathConfig::error_handler(). When we construct the App (or a ServiceConfig), we can define a custom error handler for web::Path extractors that returns custom errors. We can add it to the api_config() function, as shown in Listing 3-18.

*Listing 3-18.* Custom Error Handler for web::Path Extractor Error

```
fn api_config(cfg: &mut web::ServiceConfig) {
    cfg.service(
        web::scope("/api")
            .app_data(web::PathConfig::default().error_handler(
                |_, _| UserError::ValidationError.into(),
            ))
            .route("/cats", web::get().to(cats_endpoint))
            .route("/cat/{id}", web::get().to(cat_endpoint)),
    );
}
```

We configured a custom error handler that returns a UserError::ValidationError, which will be converted to a 400 Bad Request thanks to our ResponseError implementation.

# Logging

Good error handling helps us provide meaningful error status codes and messages to the frontend. But to really understand what happened, we need to rely on logging. When the server is small and the business logic is simple, you can easily try a few requests and reproduce a bug. But when you have thousands of concurrent users, all going through different code paths, it's hard to pinpoint where the bug is. With proper logging, you can gain visibility into what happened to the requests and easily identify problems and bugs. It might also give you a view into user behavior and trends.

There is a key concept you need to understand before jumping into logging: logging facade vs. logging implementation. A logging facade defines an "interface" for logging. A logging implementation adopts that "interface" and does the actual logging (e.g., writing to STDOUT; writing to file). A logging facade gives an extra layer of abstraction so you can swap different implementations without rewriting the whole code. This is particularly useful when building libraries. A Rust library can log using a logging facade but can't choose a concrete implementation. An application that uses libraries can choose an implementation, and as long as all the libraries adopt the same logging facade, they end up using the same implementation.

A commonly used facade is the log crate, and env_logger is a simple but effective logging implementation. The env in the name suggests that you can configure the logging level using environment variables. actix-web also provides a Logger middleware that produces access logs using the log facade.

To enable the Logger, you .wrap() the App with the Logger middleware, as shown in Listing 3-19.

**Listing 3-19.** Using the Logger Middleware

```
//...
use actix_web::middleware::Logger;
// ...

#[actix_web::main]
async fn main() -> std::io::Result<()> {
    env_logger::init();
```

```
// ...
HttpServer::new(move || {
    App::new()
        .wrap(Logger::default())
        .data(pool.clone())
        .configure(api_config)
        .service(
            Files::new("/", "static").show_files_listing(),
        )
})
.bind("127.0.0.1:8080")?
.run()
.await
}
```

The Logger middleware uses the log facade, but you need to provide a logger implementation for it to work. For that, we need to add the env_logger crate to our dependency (cargo add log env_logger) and initialize it at the beginning of main():

```
#[actix_web::main]

async fn main() -> std::io::Result<()> {
    env_logger::init();
    // ...
}
```

In the example we use Logger::default() to get the default format. But you can also customize the log format when you initialize it.

The log facade defines five log levels, ordered by priority:

- Error: Designates very serious errors.

- Warn: Designates hazardous situations.

- Info: Designates useful information.

- Debug: Designates lower priority information.

- Trace: Designates very low priority, often extremely verbose, information.

When you choose a log level, any log that has priority above or including that level will be shown. Because the env_logger's log level is configured through environment variables, we can run the server with log level set to debug in this way:

```
RUST_LOG=debug cargo run
```

When you try calling the http://localhost:8080/api/cats API, the Logger middleware should log this request[9]:

```
[2020-07-21T11:40:32Z INFO actix_server::builder] Starting 4 workers
[2020-07-21T11:40:32Z INFO actix_server::builder]
    Starting "actix-web-service-127.0.0.1:8080" service on 127.0.0.1:8080
[2020-07-21T11:41:58Z INFO actix_web::middleware::logger]
    127.0.0.1:38278 "GET /api/cats HTTP/1.1" 200 764 "-"
    "Mozilla/5.0 (X11; Linux x86_64) AppleWebKit/537.36 (KHTML, like Gecko)
    Chrome/79.0.3945.88 Safari/537.36" 0.008303
[2020-07-21T11:41:59Z DEBUG actix_files]
    Files: Failed to handle /favicon.ico: No such file or directory (os error 2)
[2020-07-21T11:41:59Z INFO actix_web::middleware::logger]
    127.0.0.1:38278 "GET /favicon.ico HTTP/1.1" 404 0
    "http://localhost:8080/api/cats" "Mozilla/5.0 (X11; Linux x86_64)
    AppleWebKit/537.36 (KHTML, like Gecko) Chrome/79.0.3945.88
    Safari/537.36" 0.000438
```

---

[9]You can see that the request for favicon.ico results in 404 Not Found. Favicon is an icon that most browsers will fetch automatically; it can be used as the icon on the browser tab, favorites list, and URL bar. We didn't add this icon, which is why you see a 404 Not Found.

You can also log custom log messages. The log crate exposes logging macros for logging at a particular level: error!(), warn!(), info!(), debug!(), and trace!(). You can add logs to all the places where errors are handled (Listing 3-20).

***Listing 3-20.*** Custom Logging

```
//...
use log::{error, info, warn};

// ...

async fn cats_endpoint(
    pool: web::Data<DbPool>,
) -> Result<HttpResponse, UserError> {
    let connection = pool.get().map_err(|_| {
        error!("Failed to get DB connection from pool");
        UserError::InternalError
    })?;

    let cats_data = web::block(move || {
        cats.limit(100).load::<Cat>(&connection)
    })
    .await
    .map_err(|_| {
        error!("Failed to get cats");
        UserError::InternalError
    })?;
    return Ok(HttpResponse::Ok().json(cats_data));
}
```

```rust
// ...

async fn cat_endpoint(
    pool: web::Data<DbPool>,
    cat_id: web::Path<CatEndpointPath>,
) -> Result<HttpResponse, UserError> {
    cat_id.validate().map_err(|_| {
        warn!("Parameter validation failed");
        UserError::ValidationError
    })?;
    let connection = pool.get().map_err(|_| {
        error!("Failed to get DB connection from pool");
        UserError::InternalError
    })?;

    let query_id = cat_id.id.clone();
    let cat_data = web::block(move || {
        cats.filter(id.eq(query_id)).first::<Cat>(&connection)
    })
    .await
    .map_err(|e| match e {
        error::BlockingError::Error(
            diesel::result::Error::NotFound,
        ) => {
            error!("Cat ID: {} not found in DB", &cat_id.id);
            UserError::NotFoundError
        }
        _ => {
            error!("Unexpected error");
            UserError::InternalError
        }
    })?;
    Ok(HttpResponse::Ok().json(cat_data))
}
```

```
// ...

#[actix_web::main]
async fn main() -> std::io::Result<()> {
    env_logger::init();
    let pool = setup_database();
    info!("Listening on port 8080");
    HttpServer::new(move || {
        App::new()
            .wrap(Logger::default())
            .data(pool.clone())
            .configure(api_config)
            .service(
                Files::new("/", "static").show_files_listing(),
            )
    })
    .bind("127.0.0.1:8080")?
    .run()
    .await
}
```

If you try to trigger a validation error (e.g., by calling curl
localhost:8080/api/cat/-1), you should see a custom log like the
following:

```
[2020-07-21T11:48:04Z INFO catdex] Listening on port 8080
[2020-07-21T11:48:04Z INFO actix_server::builder] Starting 4 workers
[2020-07-21T11:48:04Z INFO actix_server::builder]
    Starting "actix-web-service-127.0.0.1:8080" service on 127.0.0.1:8080
[2020-07-21T11:48:51Z WARN    catdex] Parameter validation failed
[2020-07-21T11:48:51Z DEBUG actix_web::middleware::logger]
    Error in response: ValidationError
```

```
[2020-07-21T11:48:51Z INFO actix_web::middleware::logger]
    127.0.0.1:38362 "GET /api/cat/-1 HTTP/1.1" 400 33 "-" "curl/7.47.0"
    0.002286
```

With carefully planned error handling and logging, you should be able to get good visibility into how your system is behaving in production.

# Enabling HTTPS

Now our API server is ready to serve the users. But we've been testing it with HTTP protocol only. To actually serve this API out on the Internet, it's important to use the HTTPS protocol, which encrypts the communication with TLS (Transport Layer Security).[10]

The first thing you need for HTTPS is a certificate for your domain name. Usually, you obtain a certificate from a Certificate Authority (CA). You can get a free certificate from Let's Encrypt[11], a non-profit CA that tries to create a more secure Web. But for the sake of demonstration, we are going to create a self-signed certificate, i.e., we'll act as our own CA and sign our own certificate.

To generate the certificate (`cert.pem`) and the private key (`key.pem`)[12], you can run this command:

```
sudo apt-get install openssl # You only need to run this once

openssl req -x509 -newkey rsa:4096 \
  -keyout key.pem \
  -out cert.pem \
```

---

[10]Formerly SSL (Secure Sockets Layer).

[11]`https://letsencrypt.org/`

[12]How HTTPS works is outside the scope of this book; you can find many good introductions online by searching for "How HTTPS works."

```
-days 365 \
-sha256 \
-subj "/CN=localhost"
```

The openssl tool will ask you to set a password for the key.pem file. If you use key.pem every time you start the actix-web server, you need to enter the password again. To remove the password, you can run

```
openssl rsa -in key.pem -out key-no-password.pem
```

This will generate a new key file called key-no-password.pem. When deploying this file to the production server, be sure to secure it with file system permissions.

Once we have the certificate and key, there are a few extra steps required for SSL:

- Install the required headers: sudo apt-get install libssl-dev.

- Add the openssl crate to the dependencies.

- Enable the openssl feature on actix-web (Listing 3-21).

***Listing 3-21.*** Enabling the openssl Feature for actix-web in Cargo.toml

```
[package]
name = "catdex"
# ...

[dependencies]
actix-web = { version = "3", features = ["openssl"] }
# ...
openssl = "0.10.30"
```

Finally, we can change our code so that the App builder uses .bind_openssl() instead of .bind(), as shown in Listing 3-22.

***Listing 3-22.***  Enabling SSL

```
// ...
use openssl::ssl::{SslAcceptor, SslFiletype, SslMethod};

// ...

#[actix_web::main]
async fn main() -> std::io::Result<()> {
    env_logger::init();

    let mut builder =
        SslAcceptor::mozilla_intermediate(SslMethod::tls())
            .unwrap();
    builder
        .set_private_key_file(
            "key-no-password.pem",
            SslFiletype::PEM,
        )
        .unwrap();
    builder.set_certificate_chain_file("cert.pem").unwrap();

    let pool = setup_database();

    info!("Listening on port 8080");
    HttpServer::new(move || {
        App::new()
            .wrap(Logger::default())
            .data(pool.clone())
            .configure(api_config)
```

```
        .service(
            Files::new("/", "static").show_files_listing(),
        )
    })
    .bind_openssl("127.0.0.1:8080", builder)?
    .run()
    .await
}
```

If you start the server with `cargo run`, you should be able to connect the website with `https://localhost:8080` instead of `http://localhost:8080`. Your browser should show a warning because it doesn't trust the self-signed CA.

# Other Alternatives

Since REST APIs can be built with almost any web framework, the frameworks presented in the previous chapter are also relevant here.

Besides REST, there are other protocols you can use to build APIs. For example, gRPC and GraphQL are some of the popular alternatives. For gRPC, there are crates like `tonic`[13] and `grpc`.[14] For GraphQL, there is `juniper`.[15] Juniper doesn't come with a web server, so it needs to be integrated into a web framework like `actix-web`.

Although JSON is one of the most popular data representation formats, you can also use other formats like XML (`serde-xml-rs`[16]) or Protobuf (`protobuf`[17] or `prost`[18]).

---

[13]https://github.com/hyperium/tonic
[14]https://github.com/stepancheg/grpc-rust
[15]https://github.com/graphql-rust/juniper
[16]https://github.com/RReverser/serde-xml-rs
[17]https://github.com/stepancheg/rust-protobuf/
[18]https://github.com/danburkert/prost

Finally, `log` allows us to log in many formats, but they are still for humans to consume. If we log in a machine-readable format (e.g., JSON), many existing log analysis tools can help us index and analyze the log. This is called *structured logging*. Currently, you can use the `slog`[19] ecosystem for structured logging. There are also efforts in introducing structured logging to `log`.[20]

---

[19]https://github.com/slog-rs/slog
[20]https://github.com/rust-lang/log/issues/149

# CHAPTER 4

# Chatting in Real-Time with WebSocket

So far, we've talked about how to send requests to an HTTP endpoint and get a response. However, under this architecture, only the client (i.e., the browser) can initiate communication. What if the server wants to notify the client about updates? What do the client and server need to be able to send messages to each other in real-time? In this chapter, we introduce another protocol called WebSocket, which provides full-duplex communication over TCP.

## Introduction to WebSocket

In the traditional HTTP model, a client (e.g., a web browser) has to initiate a request, and the server has to process that request and respond with an answer. This works well for traditional websites, which are nothing more than a collection of documents. However, as web apps become more and more interactive, people want to be able to push data from the server to the client.

One simple solution is called *polling*. A client will periodically send a request to the server to see if there is an update. The downside of this approach is very obvious: most of the time, the server won't have an update, so we waste bandwidth by sending many requests and get very little useful data in return. This might also stress out the server.

© Shing Lyu 2021

S. Lyu, *Practical Rust Web Projects*, https://doi.org/10.1007/978-1-4842-6589-5_4

A better way to achieve the same effect, but with lower overhead, is the *long polling* method. When the client sends an HTTP request to the server, the server holds the connection open until it has some data to send back. This contrasts with traditional polling, where the server responds immediately if there is no data available. Once the client receives a response, it immediately sends another request to poll for the next bit of information. Long polling reduces a lot of the overhead of polling, but the server now has the extra responsibility of keeping track of multiple open connections. It also won't work well with load balancers. To make long polling work, the load balancer usually has to use the "sticky session" strategy, which is trickier to manage than other load-balancing strategies.

Other than these hacks on top of typical HTTP requests, the HTML5 specification also has a technology called the *Server-Sent Events* (SSE). The client connects to the server using the EventSource Web API. Once the connection is established, the server can send events to the client, and the client can handle them like other DOM events. Because this method has a well-defined standard, and there are many libraries for it, the code is usually much more straightforward and readable than the long polling method. However, the data can only be sent unidirectionally (from the server to the client), which limits the use cases.

You can see a comparison of polling, long polling, and SSE in Figures 4-1 to 4-3.

Then comes WebSocket[1], the protocol we'll be discussing in this chapter. WebSocket provides full-duplex communication (i.e., it's bidirectional and messages can be sent simultaneously) over a TCP connection. The client initiates a handshake with the server using an HTTP GET request with an HTTP upgrade header. Once the server responds to the handshake, both parties upgrade to the WebSocket protocol from HTTP.

---

[1]Before WebSocket became mainstream, there were various technologies that tried to achieve similar functionality. They were collectively called *Comet*. These technologies have been made obsolete by WebSocket.

After the handshake is successful and the TCP connections are established, the client or the server can start sending messages at any time. You can find an in-depth explanation of the handshake process and the message format on MDN: `https://developer.mozilla.org/en-US/docs/Web/API/WebSockets_API/Writing_WebSocket_servers`.

WebSocket has many benefits over the methods we explained before:

- It supports real-time[2] bidirectional communication.

- It has significantly lower overhead in terms of bandwidth.

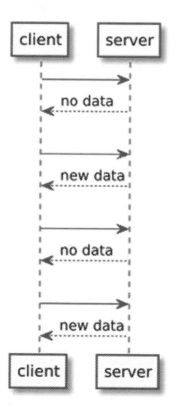

***Figure 4-1.*** *Polling*

---

[2]Real-time here means the client can get an update as soon as new information is available on the server side, rather than the client periodically checking for an update.

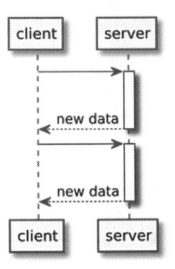

**Figure 4-2.** *Long polling*

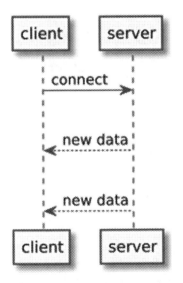

**Figure 4-3.** *SSE*

- It works on ports 80 and 443, which are the default HTTP and IITTPS ports. Therefore, it has fewer problems passing through firewalls and load balancers.

- It has standards (IETF RFC 6455 and RFC 7936).

- It has a W3C standard Web API (WebSocket), which makes it easy to implement the client-side with plain JavaScript.

# What Are You Building?

The full-duplex nature of WebSocket unlocks many use cases that were not available in the traditional client/server HTTP model. You'll be learning how to build various applications with WebSocket.

First, you'll build an echo server. An *echo server* echoes back whatever it receives from the client. It's an ideal way to start, since the echo server is very simple and it demonstrates three key actions: handshaking, sending a message from client to server, and sending a message from server to client. You'll build two clients to interact with the server, one in HTML + JavaScript, the other in Rust.

But echoing can also be done in the traditional HTTP client/server model. Therefore, you are going to build an application where the server can send notifications to the client. You'll build a WebSocket server that sends a "Meow!" message every second to any connected clients. Sometimes the client will become unresponsive; for example, the client program might hang. In such a case, the server might want to proactively disconnect the client to save bandwidth and clean up the connections. You'll build a health check system using WebSocket's ping/pong control frames to detect stale clients and disconnect them.

Finally, you'll experience the full potential of WebSocket by building a chat server. The chat server will have an HTML frontend, where multiple users can send and receive text messages in a shared chat room. You'll also expand the chat server to be able to show the user's nickname, and the time the message is sent. To send this extra information, both the client and server will have to handle structural data in JSON format.

There are many Rust implementations of the WebSocket protocol. You'll be using the `ws-rs`[3] crate, which is simple but powerful. There are many other crates that range from raw protocol implementation to a full-fledged web framework. They will be discussed in the "Other Alternatives" section later in this chapter.

# A WebSocket Echo Server

Let's start with a WebSocket echo server. The server is supposed to echo back whatever message the client sends. Before jumping into the implementation of the server, let's take a look at the client code. You are going to build an HTML and JavaScript client first, although in theory, you can build the client in any language. First, create a `client/index.html` file, as shown in Listing 4-1. The `client/index.html` file is just a simple wrapper that runs a JavaScript file called `client/index.js` (Listing 4-2).

***Listing 4-1.*** The HTML Echo Client

```
<!DOCTYPE html>
<html>
  <head>
    <meta charset="UTF-8" />
    <title>Echo client</title>
  </head>
```

---

[3]https://github.com/hausleyjk/ws-rs

```
<body>
  <script src="index.js"></script>
</body>
</html>
```

***Listing 4-2.*** The Echo Client JavaScript Code

```
const ws = new WebSocket("ws://127.0.0.1:8080")

ws.addEventListener("open", function (event) {
  console.log("Sending message to server: Meow!")
  ws.send("Meow!")
})
ws.addEventListener("message", function (event) {
  console.log("Message from server:", event.data)
})
```

There are a few interesting things to point out in this JavaScript file. First, you connect to the WebSocket server by creating a WebSocket object. The parameter you pass to the WebSocket constructor is the URL to the server. The URL uses the ws:// protocol, instead of the commonly used http://. There is also an https:// equivalent called WebSocket Secure, wss://. For the ease of development, you are going to run the server on your own computer (with the 127.0.0.1 loopback IP) and a special port 8080.

After the WebSocket object is created, you can attach event handlers to it. There are four types of events:

- open: Connection established

- message: Received message from the server

- error: Error happened

- close: Connection closed

For this simple example, you can send a message in the open event handler. When WebSocket establishes the connection, it will call the open handler and send a message using ws.send(). The message is a simple string, "Meow!".

After the server receives the message and echoes back, the incoming message triggers the message event. You can set up a second event handler to print out the server's response (stored in event.data) using console.log().

Now that you understand how the client is going to interact with the server, how should you write the Rust server to actually handle the request? First, create a binary Rust project by running cargo new echo-server in the command line. Then add the ws crate to the Cargo.toml file (Listing 4-3).

***Listing 4-3.*** Cargo.toml for echo-server

```
[package]
name = "echo-server"
edition = "2018"

[dependencies]
ws = "0.9.1"
```

Once you declare the dependency, open the src/main.rs file and add the code in Listing 4-4.

***Listing 4-4.*** Echo Server

```
extern crate ws;

fn main() {
    ws::listen("127.0.0.1:8080", |out| {
        move |msg| {
            println!("Received message: {}", msg);
```

```
            out.send(msg)
        }
    })
    .unwrap()
}
```

---

**Note**   The examples in this chapter mostly consist of one src/main.rs file. If you are following along, you can simply replace the src/main.rs file for each example. But in the example code repository, all these example files are placed in the examples folder so they can coexist. To run a particular example, you run cargo run--example <name of example>. For example, the echo server example can be executed by running cargo run --example echo_server. We include the command needed to run each example in the footnotes.

---

The intention of the code is apparent:

- Starts a TCP server that listens on the address 127.0.0.1:8080.

- Whenever a client's message (msg) arrives, echoes it back using out.send().

But you might find the two layers of closures confusing. Why do we need an outer closure and an inner closure with move? For that, you'll need to know how ws-rs works.

In order for ws-rs to be able to handle 100,000+ connections on a single thread, ws-rs uses asynchronous I/O just like Actix. It uses mio, a low-level IO library that is part of the Tokio project. The outer closure implements the Factory trait. When a TCP connection is created, ws-rs will create a request handler (i.e., the inner closure), which implements the trait Handler, to handle this request. The out parameter in the outer closure has the type Sender. It provides a send() function, which can be used to send the response back.

The Handler trait defines various functions to handle WebSocket events. To highlight a few examples:

- on_open(): WebSocket connection opened

- on_message(): Receives message from the client

- on_error(): Error happens

- on_close(): WebSocket connection closed

ws-rs implements Handler on the type Fn(Message) -> Result<()>, so we can use a closure as a Handler. The closure will be used as the on_message(), because it's the most used method in most cases. Therefore, the inner closure move |msg| {...} is the Handler. It receives a Message (the msg parameter) and echoes the message back with out.send(msg). Because multiple clients can connect to the server and call the Factory multiple times, the Handler needs to take ownership of the variables it uses. That's why we need to have a move for the Handler closure.

To test this server, you can start the server by running cargo run.[4] Then you can open the index.html file in a web browser. To see the logs from JavaScript, you'll need to open the developer console of your browser.

---

**Note**   Here is how you can open the developer console:

- Google Chrome

  - Click the menu button (the vertically stacked three dots icon).

---

[4]cargo run --example echo_server in the example code.

- Select More Tools ➤ Developer Tools.

- Select the Console tab.

- Firefox

  - Click the menu button (the vertically stacked three lines icon).

  - Select ➤ Web Developer ➤ Toggle Tools.

  - Select the Console tab.

You should be able to see the log output in the developer tool, similar to Figure 4-4.

# Pushing Notifications from the Server

In the echo server example, it's still the client who initiates the communication. To see the real power of WebSocket, we are going to build a push notification server that can send periodic notifications to the client, without the client explicitly asking for one. For this server, we'll open a WebSocket server, and then we'll start a new thread that periodically sends messages through this server. You can change the source code to Listing 4-5.

*Listing 4-5.* Push Notification Server

```
extern crate ws;

use std::{thread, time};
use ws::{Handler, Sender, WebSocket};

struct Server {
    out: Sender,
}
```

```
// Implement Handler and use all the default implementation
impl Handler for Server {}

fn main() {
    let server = WebSocket::new(|out| Server { out }).unwrap();

    let broadcaster = server.broadcaster();

    let periodic = thread::spawn(move || loop {
        broadcaster.send("Meow!").unwrap();
        thread::sleep(time::Duration::from_secs(1));
    });

    server.listen("127.0.0.1:8080").unwrap();

    // Block on the periodic thread to avoid to exit right away
    periodic.join().unwrap();
}
```

A few things changed in this example. First, in the beginning of the main() function, you call WebSocket::new() to create a WebSocket instance, instead of directly calling ws::listen(). You then call the server.listen() function near the end of the main() function.

The Factory closure you pass to WebSocket::new() returns a Server struct instead of a closure. The Server, defined right before the main function, is a struct that only holds the Sender. You also implement Handler on it without any custom function implementation, so it gets the default implementation from Handler.

**Figure 4-4.** *Echo client log output*

This gives us the flexibility to customize various event handlers in later sections.

Once you initialize the WebSocket and store it in a variable named server, how do you send push notifications to all clients? You can call server.broadcaster() to get the broadcaster. The broadcaster gives you the ability to send a message to all connected clients at once.

To keep sending the messages over and over again, you can start a new thread using thread::spawn(). The spawned thread runs an infinite loop, which broadcasts a "Meow!" string every second.

Now you can test the server by following these steps:

- Start the server with cargo run.[5]

- Open the client HTML file.

- Open the developer console.

You should see that the console prints out the message received every second (Figure 4-5).

---

[5]cargo run --example push_notification in the example code.

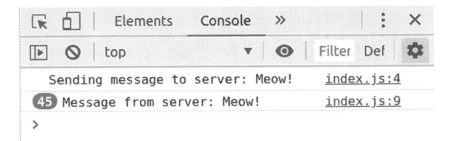

**Figure 4-5.** *Client receiving push notifications*

This example can be expanded to solve many different use cases. You can replace the thread that periodically sends messages to any kind of event source or input. Some example use cases include:

- When new data is added to a database, you can send a message to a frontend dashboard to update the graphs.

- When a long-running job is finished, you can send a message to the website's notification center.

- When a message is added to a queue, you can broadcast it to all the subscribed clients.

# Cleaning Up Unresponsive Clients

Sometimes, a client becomes unresponsive. The client code might run into an infinite loop. Or it might hang, but the connection is kept open. These unresponsive clients occupy precious TCP connections and bandwidth, wasting resources on the server side. If the server can detect such clients and proactively disconnect them, the server can allocate the resources to other responsive clients.

To detect an unresponsive client, the server can use a pattern commonly used in distributed systems, the *heartbeat*. The server can periodically send a message to the client and ask the client to respond immediately. If the client fails to respond to a few consecutive heartbeat messages, the server can assume the client is not responsive. The good news is that you don't have to implement this heartbeat message format yourself. The WebSocket protocol defines two particular message formats (a.k.a., control frames): *ping* and *pong*.

---

**Note**    The "message" in WebSocket is not just a plain string. The WebSocket standard defines a "frame" format.[6] In a frame, there are a few metadata fields that tell the recipient how the data should be interpreted. One of the metadata fields is the 4-bit *opcode* (an abbreviation of *operation code*). The opcode indicates how the payload should be interpreted. Commonly used opcodes include:

- 0x1: Text (UTF-8 encoded)

- 0x2: Binary

- 0x9: Ping

- 0xA: Pong

This is why we say the ping and pong frames are special control frames.

---

When a client or server receives a ping, it should reply with a pong with the exact same payload in the ping. Most modern web browsers' WebSocket implementations implement this protocol, so if you send a ping to a JavaScript client running in the browser, it should respond with a pong without you having to write any extra code.

---

[6]https://tools.ietf.org/html/rfc6455#page-28

To detect unresponsive clients, you need to make a few changes to the existing server:

1.  Set a five-second timer (the ping timer) when a connection is open. Ping the client when the timer expires and immediately schedule another five-second timer, so you ping the client every five seconds.

2.  Set a 15-second timer (the unresponsive timer) when a connection is open. Whenever the server receives a pong, reset this timer.

3.  If the unresponsive timer expires because the client is not ponging back, close the connection to that client.

The simple way of defining the Handler as a closure is very handy if you only need the on_message() handler. But to send periodic pings, you need to utilize other event handlers like on_frame(), on_connect() and on_timeout(). This is when the impl Handler for Server in Listing 4-5 comes in handy.

Let's first implement the ping timer that triggers a ping every five seconds. You need to add a few event handlers to the impl Handler for Server part, as shown in Listing 4-6.

*Listing 4-6.* The Five-Second Ping Timer

```
extern crate ws;

use std::{thread, time};
use ws::util::{Timeout, Token};
use ws::{
    CloseCode, Error, ErrorKind, Handler, Handshake,
    Result, Sender, WebSocket,
};
```

```rust
const PING: Token = Token(0);

struct Server {
    out: Sender,
    ping_timeout: Option<Timeout>,
}

impl Handler for Server {
    fn on_open(&mut self, _: Handshake) -> Result<()> {
        self.out.timeout(5_000, PING)
    }

    fn on_timeout(&mut self, event: Token) -> Result<()> {
        match event {
            PING => {
                println!("Pinging the client");
                self.out.ping("".into())?;
                self.out.timeout(5_000, PING)
            }
            _ => Err(Error::new(
                ErrorKind::Internal,
                "Invalid timeout token encountered!",
            )),
        }
    }

    fn on_new_timeout(
        &mut self,
        event: Token,
        timeout: Timeout,
    ) -> Result<()> {
        match event {
            PING => {
```

```rust
                if let Some(timeout) =
                    self.ping_timeout.take() {
                    self.out.cancel(timeout)?
                }
                self.ping_timeout = Some(timeout);
            }
            _ => {
                eprintln!("Unknown event: {:?}", event);
            }
        }
    }
    Ok(())
}

fn on_close(&mut self, code: CloseCode, reason: &str) {
    println!(
        "WebSocket closing for ({:?}) {}",
        code, reason
    );

    if let Some(timeout) = self.ping_timeout.take() {
        self.out.cancel(timeout).unwrap()
    }
}
}

fn main() {
    let server = WebSocket::new(|out| Server {
        out: out,
        ping_timeout: None,
    })
    .unwrap();

    let broadcaster = server.broadcaster();
```

```
let periodic = thread::spawn(move || loop {
    broadcaster.send("Meow").unwrap();
    thread::sleep(time::Duration::from_secs(1));
});
server.listen("127.0.0.1:8080").unwrap();
periodic.join().unwrap();
}
```

When a new client connects, that event triggers the on_open() handler. Inside the handler, you can start a timer using the timeout() method of the Sender type. This will create a timer on the underlying mio event loop. The first parameter is the milliseconds you want it to wait, which is set to 5000. The second parameter is a Token. This token will help identify different timers when we add another one later. You can create a token called PING before this function, near the beginning of the file.

When the five second (5000 milliseconds) time period is over, it will trigger the on_timeout() handler. In that handler, you can match against the Token to know which timer is triggering this event. When you see that a PING timer has expired, you can send a ping to the client using self.out.ping(). You can optionally assign a payload to it, but in this example, we only use an empty string. Right after you sent the ping, remember to set another timeout so that it will send another ping five seconds later.

Since the timers are running asynchronously, it's very easy to accidentally create multiple timers, which will cause a lot of pain to debug. You can safeguard against that by monitoring the new_timeout event. This event will be triggered when you try to schedule a new timeout. You'll need to create a new field (ping_timeout) in the Server struct to hold the current timer. This field has a type of Option<Timeout>; when it's set to None, we know there is no running timer. In the on_new_timeout() handler, you can first check if there is a running timer stored in self.ping_timeout. If so, cancel the self.ping_timeout and assign the newly created timer to the self.ping_timeout field. This ensures that only one timer is running at any instant.

Finally don't forget to clear self.ping_timeout when the client closes the connection (i.e., in on_close()). This ensures that the server stops sending pings to disconnected clients.

To test this code, simply run cargo run[7]. Then open the client/index.html file in a browser, and you should be able to see the server logging "Pinging the client" every five seconds.

At this point, the server sends a ping every five seconds, but it doesn't do anything against unresponsive clients. You might not want to disconnect the client immediately after it fails to respond to one ping. Sometimes the network is flaky, so one dropped ping or pong is normal. Therefore, you can set a longer timer for identifying the client as unresponsive. For example, if the unresponsive timer is set to 15 seconds, it will take roughly three failed pongs for the client to be considered unresponsive. Whenever a pong is received, this timer will be reset and will start the countdown from 15 seconds again.

The unresponsive timer is created in a similar way as the ping timer, but it gets a different Token, as shown in Listing 4-7.

*Listing 4-7.* The Unresponsive Timer

```
extern crate ws;

use std::{thread, time};
use ws::util::{Timeout, Token};
use ws::{
    CloseCode, Error, ErrorKind, Frame, Handler, Handshake,
    OpCode, Result, Sender, WebSocket,
};

const PING: Token = Token(0);
const CLIENT_UNRESPONSIVE: Token = Token(1);
```

---

[7]cargo run --example 5 sec ping timer in the example code.

```rust
struct Server {
    out: Sender,
    ping_timeout: Option<Timeout>,
    client_unresponsive_timeout: Option<Timeout>,
}
impl Handler for Server {
    fn on_open(&mut self, _: Handshake) -> Result<()> {
        println!("Opened a connection");
        self.out.timeout(15_000, CLIENT_UNRESPONSIVE)?;
        self.out.timeout(5_000, PING)
    }

    fn on_timeout(&mut self, event: Token) -> Result<()> {
        println!("event: {:?}", event);
        match event {
            PING => {
                println!("Pinging the client");
                self.out.ping("".into())?;
                match self.client_unresponsive_timeout {
                    Some(_) => self.out.timeout(5_000, PING),
                    None => Ok(()), // skip
                }
            }
            CLIENT_UNRESPONSIVE => {
                println!("Client is unresponsive, \
                            closing the connection");

                self.client_unresponsive_timeout.take();
                if let Some(timeout) =
                    self.ping_timeout.take() {
                    println!("timeout: {:?}", timeout);
```

```rust
                self.out.cancel(timeout)?;
                println!("canceled");
            }

            self.out.close(CloseCode::Away)
        }
        _ => Err(Error::new(
            ErrorKind::Internal,
            "Invalid timeout token encountered!",
        )),
    }
}

fn on_new_timeout(
    &mut self,
    event: Token,
    timeout: Timeout,
) -> Result<()> {
    println!("new timeout: {:?}", timeout);
    match event {
        PING => {
            if let Some(timeout) =
                self.ping_timeout.take()     {
                self.out.cancel(timeout)?
            }
            match self.client_unresponsive_timeout {
                Some(_) => {
                    self.ping_timeout = Some(timeout),
                }
                None => self.ping_timeout = None,
            }
        }
```

```rust
        CLIENT_UNRESPONSIVE => {
            if let Some(timeout) =
                self.client_unresponsive_timeout.take()
            {
                self.out.cancel(timeout)?;
            }
            self.client_unresponsive_timeout =
                Some(timeout)
        }
        _ => {
            eprintln!("Unknown event: {:?}", event);
        }
    }
    }
    Ok(())
}

fn on_frame(
    &mut self,
    frame: Frame,
) -> Result<Option<Frame>> {
    if frame.opcode() == OpCode::Pong {
        println!("Received a pong");
        // Reset the CLIENT_UNRESPONSIVE timeout
        self.out.timeout(15_000, CLIENT_UNRESPONSIVE)?;
    }

    Ok(Some(frame))
}

fn on_close(&mut self, code: CloseCode, reason: &str) {
    println!(
        "WebSocket closing for ({:?}) {}",
        code, reason
    );
```

```rust
        if let Some(timeout) = self.ping_timeout.take() {
            self.out.cancel(timeout).unwrap()
        }
    }
}

fn main() {
    let server = WebSocket::new(|out| Server {
        out: out,
        ping_timeout: None,
        client_unresponsive_timeout: None,
    })
    .unwrap();
    let broadcaster = server.broadcaster();

    let periodic = thread::spawn(move || loop {
        broadcaster.send("Meow").unwrap();
        thread::sleep(time::Duration::from_secs(1));
    });
    server.listen("127.0.0.1:8080").unwrap();
    periodic.join().unwrap();
}
```

The most critical addition to Listing 4-6 is the on_frame() handler.
When the server receives the pong control frame, which can be identified
by its opcode, it will create a new CLIENT_UNRESPONSIVE timer. Then,
in the on_new_timeout() handler, you can cancel the current active
Server.client_unresponsive_timeout and replace it with the new one.
This effectively resets the unresponsive timer.

You also need to change how the ping timer is handled in
on_timeout() and on_new_timeout(). Because the ping timer and
unresponsive timer might not be in sync, when the ping timer expires, the
unresponsive timer might have already expired. In that scenario, the client

is already being treated as unresponsive, so there is no point in pinging it again. Therefore, before scheduling a new ping timer, the server should check if `self.client_unresponsive_timeout` is set to None. If it's None, it should not schedule another ping timer.

Currently, `ws-rs` doesn't support forcefully disconnecting a particular connection. The best you can do is to call `self.out.close(CloseCode::Away)`, hoping that the client will receive it and close the connection properly. If the client does not close, you can only stop interacting with the client and wait for the connection to be dropped because of a connection timeout.

# Two-Way Chat

All the examples you've seen can be implemented in alternative technologies:

- Echo server: HTTP RESTful API

- Push notification server: Server-Sent Events (SSE)

The true strength of WebSocket lies in its full-duplex capability. One of the most common use cases for a full-duplex connection is an online text chat. You can build a chat room quickly with `ws-rs`. You are going to build a public chat room, where every user connects to the same room and can talk to everybody.

You can create a new project following the same steps as in the previous examples:

- Create a project with `cargo new chat`.

- Add `ws = "0.9.1"` to the [dependencies] section in `Cargo.toml`.

- Copy and paste the code in Listing 4-8 into the `src/main.rs`.

*Listing 4-8.* A Minimal Chat Server

```
extern crate ws;

fn main() {
    ws::listen("127.0.0.1:8080", |out| {
        move |msg| {
            println!("Received message: {}", msg);
            out.broadcast(msg)
        }
    })
    .unwrap()
}
```

You might notice that the code in Listing 4-8 looks almost the same as the echo server code in Listing , except that the out.send() line is replaced with out.broadcast(). Instead of replying individually to each client, the server now broadcasts whatever message it receives to all the clients.

Now you need to build a frontend for this chat room. First, create a file named chat.html and paste the code in Listing 4-9 into it.

*Listing 4-9.* HTML for Chat Frontend

```
<!DOCTYPE html>
<html>
  <head>
    <meta charset="utf-8">
    <title>WebSocket Chat</title>
    <style type="text/css">
    #messages {
      width: 95vw;
      height: 80vh;
    }
```

```
  #message {
    width: 80vw;
  }
  </style>
</head>
<body>
  <textarea name="messages" id="messages"></textarea>
  <input type="text" id="message"></textarea>
  <button id="send">Send</button>

  <script src="chat.js" charset="utf-8"></script>
</body>
</html>
```

This HTML defines four elements in its body:

- `<textarea>`: The box that displays all the chat messages from every participant.

- `<input>`: The text box to type in your message.

- `<button>`: The button to submit your message.

- `<script src="chat.js">`: The JavaScript file that contains the logic, which will be discussed later.

There is also some CSS in the `<head>` section so the `<textarea>` and `<input>` will make the best use of the available screen space. When you open the chat.html file in a browser, it should look like Figure 4-6.

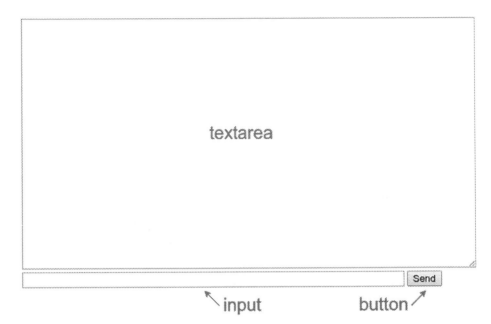

*Figure 4-6.* *Chat frontend*

You can now create another file, called chat.js, alongside chat.html. The contents of the file are shown in Listing 4-10.

*Listing 4-10.* chat.js

```
document.addEventListener("DOMContentLoaded", function(){
  const socket = new WebSocket("ws://127.0.0.1:8080");

  socket.onmessage = function (event) {
    // #messages is the <textarea/>
    const messages = document.getElementById("messages");
    // Append the received message
    // to the existing list of messages
    messages.value += '${event.data}\n';
  };
```

```
const sendButton= document.getElementById("send");
sendButton.addEventListener("click", (event) => {
  // #message is the <input/>
  const message = document.getElementById("message");
  socket.send(message.value)
  message.value = ""; // Clear the input box
})
});
```

All the code in Listing 4-10 is wrapped in an event handler for the DOMContentLoaded event. That is because if the DOM element is not ready, a call to document.getElementById() will not find the element. Therefore, we have to wait until all the DOM elements are loaded before we do anything else.

The first thing you do inside the DOMContentLoaded event handler is connect to the WebSocket server address ws://127.0.0.1:8080. Once the connection is established, you can set an onmessage event handler on it. The event handler will append the received message to the <textarea/>, which we get by document.getElementById("messages").

You also need to add an event handler to the <button/>, so it will send the message when being clicked. The click event handler on the button reads the value of the <input/> and sends it to the WebSocket server. Finally, it clears the <input/>, so the user can start typing the next messages.

If you start the server with cargo run[8] and then open the chat.html in two browser windows, you'll now be able to send a message across the browser windows (Figure 4-7).

---

[8]cargo run --example chat server in the example code.

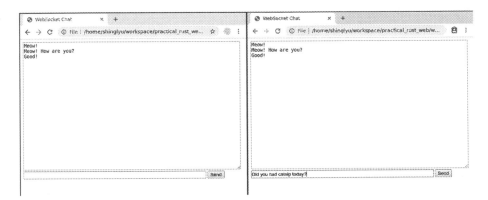

***Figure 4-7.***  *Chatting across two browser windows*

# Sending Structural JSON Data

The chat application you just built is lacking a few features commonly found in chat apps:

- Showing the sender of the message

- Showing when the message is sent (or received by the server)

Currently, the only message sent between the client and server is the message text. But to also carry the information about the sender and time, you'll need to send structural data like JSON. ws-rs can easily send serialized JSON strings. To make it easier to serialize and deserialize the JSON strings, you'll be using the serde and serde_json crates.

To show the sender, we have to send the sender's name along with the text message. The format should be a JSON structure like this:

```
{
    name: "Simba",
    message: "Meow!"
}
```

To let the users choose their own names, you can use the `window.prompt()` (`prompt()` for short) to ask users for their preferred nickname. We can slightly tweak the code in Listing 4-10 into Listing 4-11.

***Listing 4-11.*** Use `prompt()` to Ask for User Nicknames

```
document.addEventListener("DOMContentLoaded", function(){
    const name = prompt("What is your name?")
    document.getElementById("name").innerText = name;
});
```

You can also add a `<span id="name"/>` in front of the `<input/>` to show the user's chosen nickname, as shown in Listing 4-12. The code in Listing 4-11 sets the name as the `innerText` for this span.

***Listing 4-12.*** HTML for the JSON Chat Client

```
<!DOCTYPE html>
<html>
  <head>
    <meta charset="utf-8">
    <title>WebSocket Chat</title>
    <style type="text/css">
      /* ... */
    </style>
  </head>
  <body>
    <textarea name="messages" id="messages"></textarea>
    <span id="name"></span> <!-- show the name -->
    <input type="text" id="message"></input>
    <button id="send">Send</button>

    <script src="chat.js" charset="utf-8"></script>
  </body>
</html>
```

Once you have the user's name, you can change the submit button's click handler so it sends the JSON format instead of just the text message. This is shown in Listing 4-13.

*Listing 4-13.* Sending the JSON Message Including the Name

```
document.addEventListener("DOMContentLoaded", function(){
    const name = prompt("What is your name?")
    document.getElementById("name").innerText = name;

    const socket = new WebSocket("ws://localhost:8080");

    // socket.onmessage will be implemented later

    const sendButton= document.getElementById("send");
    sendButton.addEventListener("click", (event) => {
        const message = document.getElementById("message");
        socket.send(
            JSON.stringify({
                name: name,
                message: message.value
            })
        )
        message.value = "";
    })
});
```

How can the server parse this JSON string in the backend and manipulate it as a Rust struct? You'll have to use the serde, serde_json and serde_derive crates. Add these dependencies to your Cargo.toml file, as shown in Listing 4-14.

***Listing 4-14.*** `Cargo.toml` for the JSON Chat Server

```
[package]
# ...

[dependencies]
ws = "0.9.1"
serde = "1.0.104"
serde_json = "1.0.48"
serde_derive = "1.0.104"
```

Then in the code (Listing 4-15), we can define a struct to represent the JSON format we are expecting. You need to derive the `Serialize` and `Deserialize` traits on this struct, so we can use the following code to serialize and deserialize this JSON format:

- `serde_json::from_str()`: Takes a &str and deserializes it to a `JSONMessage` structure.

- `json!()`: Takes a `JSONMessage` structure and serializes it.

***Listing 4-15.*** Defining the JSON Struct Format

```
extern crate serde;
#[macro_use]
extern crate serde_json;
#[macro_use]
extern crate serde_derive;

#[derive(Serialize, Deserialize)]
struct JSONMessage {
    name: String,
    message: String,
}
```

In the main() function, you can write a handler that is similar to the chat server in the previous section. But you'll need to do a few extra things other than just broadcast the received message:

1.  Deserialize the received JSON object into a JSONMessage struct.

2.  Get the current time.

3.  Construct a new struct with all the fields in the JSONMessage, plus the time.

4.  Serialize the new struct and broadcast it to the clients.

With help from serde, the serialization and deserialization code is very simple, as shown in Listing 4-16.

***Listing 4-16.*** The Main Handler for the JSON Chat Server

```
extern crate serde;
extern crate ws;
#[macro_use]
extern crate serde_json;
#[macro_use]
extern crate serde_derive;

use std::time::{SystemTime, UNIX_EPOCH};
use ws::{listen, Message};

#[derive(Serialize, Deserialize)]
struct JSONMessage {
    name: String,
    message: String,
}
```

```rust
fn main() {
    listen("127.0.0.1:8080", |out| {
        move |msg: Message| {
            let msg_text = msg.as_text().unwrap();
            if let Ok(json_message) =
                serde_json::from_str::<JSONMessage>(msg_text)
            {
                let now = SystemTime::now()
                    .duration_since(UNIX_EPOCH)
                    .expect("Time went backwards");
                println!(
                    "{} said: {} at {:?}",
                    json_message.name,
                    json_message.message,
                    now.as_millis()
                );
                let output_msg = json!({
                    "name": json_message.name,
                    "message": json_message.message,
                    "received_at": now.as_millis().to_string()
                });

                out.broadcast(Message::Text(
                    output_msg.to_string(),
                ))?;
            }
            Ok(())
        }
    })
    .unwrap();
}
```

You'll notice that the message is converted to a &str using as_text(), because the serde_json::from_str() can only accept str. Then the msg_text is deserialized into the JSONMessage struct.

To get the time, you can use the std::time::SystemTime::now() function. This returns a SystemTime struct, which is not very friendly for the serializer. Therefore, you can convert it to a UNIX timestamp by using duration_since(UNIX_EPOCH).

---

**Note**    The *UNIX time* is a common way to describe a moment in time in computer systems. The definition of UNIX time is the number of seconds since the 00:00:00 UTC on 1 January 1970, called the *UNIX epoch*. This way of describing time as a single number works well with JSON serialization and deserialization. Both Rust's SystemTime and JavaScript's Date can work with this representation nicely.

---

Then, you use the json!() macro to construct a new serde_json::Value. This Value will contain the name, message, and the received_at timestamp, which we set to the current time (in UNIX epoch milliseconds). Finally, you can call out.broadcast() to broadcast the message. Notice that we call output_msg.to_string() to the Value, which is serialized to a string right before sending.

Once the client receives the broadcast, it can deserialize the JSON message and display it properly. You can add the WebSocket message handler to the code in Listing 4-13, as shown in Listing 4-17.

***Listing 4-17.*** Receiving and Displaying the JSON Message

```
document.addEventListener("DOMContentLoaded", function(){
    const name = prompt("What is your name?")
    document.getElementById("name").innerText = name;

    const socket = new WebSocket("ws://localhost:8080");
```

```
socket.onmessage = function (event) {
    const messages = document.getElementById("messages");
    const msg = JSON.parse(event.data);
    const time = (new Date(Number(msg.received_at)))
        .toLocaleString("en-US")
    messages.value +=
        '[${time}] ${msg.name}: ${msg.message}\n';
};

const sendButton= document.getElementById("send");
sendButton.addEventListener("click", (event) => {
    // ...
})
});
```

In the `socket.onmessage` handler, you parse the JSON string into a
JavaScript object with `JSON.parse()`. The time is converted from the UNIX
milliseconds timestamp into a JavaScript `Date` object first, then converted
to a human-readable string using `Date.toLocaleString("en-US")`.
Finally, you can format the message into the following format and append
it to the `<textarea/>`:

```
[8/8/2020, 8:00:00 PM] Simba: Meow!
```

A complete working example will look like Figure 4-8.

***Figure 4-8.*** *JSON chat in action*

# Other Alternatives

There are a few WebSocket implementations in Rust, besides ws-rs. The most active ones are:

- tungstenite[9]: This crate uses the mio event loop, the same as ws-rs. Although it was created after ws-rs, the development momentum seems to be high. There is also a tokio-tungstenite[10] crate, which you can use in Tokio, a high-level async I/O runtime on top of mio.

- actix-web[11]: actix-web is not just a WebSocket library. It's a full-fledged web framework building on the Actix actor framework. You can build common HTTP/HTTPS web servers and also WebSocket servers with it. If you are building a big web service with WebSocket functionality, give Actix a try.

---

[9]https://crates.io/crates/tungstenite
[10]https://crates.io/crates/tokio-tungstenite
[11]https://crates.io/crates/actix-web

There are also a few less active ones. Although they might not be actively maintained anymore, it's interesting to compare their implementation to others if you are into the WebSocket protocol itself:

- websocket[12]

- twist[13]

- soketto[14], which is a fork of twist

---

[12]https://crates.io/crates/websocket
[13]https://crates.io/crates/twist
[14]https://crates.io/crates/soketto

# CHAPTER 5

# Going Serverless

We built a website, a REST API, and WebSocket servers in the previous chapters. They work fine when you run them on your local machine and test them with low traffic. But when you need to make them publicly accessible, managing the server becomes a headache. Traditionally you'll have to buy physical servers and run your applications on them. You'll have to take care of every aspect of it, from keeping the operating system and system libraries up-to-date, to making sure failed hardware is replaced, and keeping the servers powered even when there is a power outage. Unless you have a big budget and an operations team, this is not a fun job.

If you don't want to handle these troubles yourself, there are many companies that let you outsource their servers. For example, third-party web hosting and virtual private server (VPS) services have existed for a long time. Nowadays, you also have many Infrastructure-as-a-Service (IaaS) and Platform-as-a-Service (PaaS) providers you can choose from. They manage the servers for you and provide different levels of abstraction, so you can focus on your application. Serverless computing pushes this idea to the extreme. With serverless computing, you just write the functions that handle the business logic. The hardware, OS, and the language runtime are all handled by the service provider. You can also connect them to managed databases, message queues, and file storage, which are also fully managed by the service provider.

Most of the big cloud providers offer some form of serverless computing capability. In this chapter, we'll use Amazon Web Service's (AWS) Lambda as our computation platform. We'll also use DynamoDB, a fully managed NoSQL database from AWS.

© Shing Lyu 2021
S. Lyu, *Practical Rust Web Projects*, https://doi.org/10.1007/978-1-4842-6589-5_5

# What Are You Building?

In this chapter, you are going to rebuild the Catdex REST API again in a serverless fashion. You'll learn to build the following features:

- Run Rust code on an AWS Lambda.

- Create a REST API endpoint using the Serverless Application Framework.

- Use the `lambda_http` crate to handle API requests coming from AWS API Gateway.

- Read from DynamoDB through the `Rusoto` AWS SDK.

- Write to DynamoDB to create a new cat.

- Upload images directly to S3, an object storage service for storing files.

- Serve the frontend from S3.

- Enable Cross-Origin Resource Sharing (CORS) so the frontend can access the API.

# Registering an AWS Account

Since we are going to run our service on Amazon Web Service (AWS), you need to register an account. Visit `https://aws.amazon.com` in your browser and click the Create an AWS Account button. Follow the steps and sign up for an account. You might need to provide a credit card during the process.

AWS provides one year of free-tier services (usage limitations apply) when you sign up for the first time. This covers most of the services we are going to use: Lambda, DynamoDB, and S3. Therefore, you should be able to run most of the examples with minimal to no cost. But remember to clean up all the resources after you finish testing.

# Hello World in Lambda

AWS Lambda is a service that allows you to run code without provisioning a server. AWS manages the underlying hardware, networking, operating system, and runtime. As a developer, you only upload a piece of code and it can run and scale automatically. A lambda function can be triggered manually (via the web console or AWS CLI), or by events generated by other AWS services. For REST APIs, it's common to use API Gateway or Application Load Balancer to handle the request and trigger the lambda.

AWS Lambda frees developers from configuring and managing the servers, so they can focus on the code. You are charged by the compute time you consume, so if your function is sitting idle, you don't pay anything. Lambda can also scale automatically. If you use Lambda to power a REST API, it can automatically spin up more lambda instances when traffic is high.

AWS Lambda provides many language runtimes like Java, Go, PowerShell, Node.js, C, Python, and Ruby. It also provides a Runtime API so you can build your custom runtime[1]. AWS has released an experimental runtime for Rust using this runtime mechanism, so we can run Rust code on Lambda.

---

**Note**   The underlying technology that powers AWS Lambda is Firecracker VM.[2] Interestingly, Firecracker VM is written in Rust. So even if you write lambdas in other languages, your code is still powered by Rust. The project is released as an open source project by AWS. You can find ways to contribute to it by visiting its GitHub repository: `https://github.com/firecracker-microvm/firecracker`.

---

[1]See `https://docs.aws.amazon.com/lambda/latest/dg/runtimes-custom.html`.
[2]`https://firecracker-microvm.github.io/`

The first thing we are going to look at is the Hello World lambda
from the AWS official blog.[3] We are going to deploy this lambda and test
it through the AWS management console. First, create a Rust project by
running `cargo new serverless-hello-world --bin` and `cd` into the
`serverless-hello-world` folder. Then you need to add the `lambda_runtime`
crate by using `cargo add lambda_runtime`. There are also some extra
dependencies for JSON serialization/deserialization and logging, so you
need to add them to the dependency section of `Cargo.toml` as well:

```
lambda_runtime = "0.2.1"
serde = "^1"
serde_json = "^1"
serde_derive = "^1"
tokio = "0.1"
log = "^0.4"
simple_logger = "^1"
simple-error = "^0.1"
```

When you use AWS Lambda custom runtime, the Lambda service
will look for a binary named `bootstrap` and execute it when the lambda is
triggered. Therefore, we need to add the following lines to your `Cargo.toml`,
so when you run `cargo build`, it will compile `src/main.rs` as a binary
called `bootstrap`:

```
[[bin]]
name = "bootstrap"
path = "src/main.rs"
```

Now your `Cargo.toml` file should look like Listing 5-1.

---

[3]`https://aws.amazon.com/blogs/opensource/rust-runtime-for-aws-lambda/`

***Listing 5-1.*** Cargo.toml for the Hello World Example

```
[package]
name - "serverless-hello-world"
version = "0.1.0"
authors = ["Shing Lyu"]
edition = "2018"

# See more keys and their definitions at
# https://doc.rust-lang.org/cargo/reference/manifest.html

[dependencies]
lambda_runtime = "0.2.1"
serde = "^1"
serde_json = "^1"
serde_derive = "^1"
tokio = "0.1"
log = "^0.4"
simple_logger = "^1.11"
simple-error = "^0.1"

[[bin]]
name = "bootstrap"
path = "src/main.rs"
```

With the dependencies in place, we can look at the code. Copy Listing 5-2 into src/main.rs.

***Listing 5-2.*** main.rs for the Hello World Example

```
use std::error::Error;

use lambda_runtime::{error::HandlerError, lambda, Context};
use log::{self, error};
use serde_derive::{Deserialize, Serialize};
use simple_error::bail;
use simple_logger::SimpleLogger;
```

```rust
#[derive(Deserialize)]
struct CustomEvent {
    #[serde(rename = "firstName")]
    first_name: String,
}

#[derive(Serialize)]
struct CustomOutput {
    message: String,
}

fn main() -> Result<(), Box<dyn Error>> {
    SimpleLogger::new().with_level(log::LevelFilter::Debug)
        .init()?;
    lambda!(my_handler);

    Ok(())
}

fn my_handler(
    e: CustomEvent,
    c: Context,
) -> Result<CustomOutput, HandlerError> {
    if e.first_name == "" {
        error!(
            "Empty first name in request {}",
            c.aws_request_id
        );
        bail!("Empty first name");
    }

    Ok(CustomOutput {
        message: format!("Hello, {}!", e.first_name),
    })
}
```

In the main function, you can see we set up a simple_logger for logging. The log generated by the lambda will be collected in AWS CloudWatch, AWS's logging and metrics service. Then we use the lambda! macro to mark the my_handler() function as the lambda handler. That means when an event triggers the lambda, it will call the my_handler() function and pass the event and some context information.

A lambda can handle different types of events from different sources, like API Gateway, SQS, S3 or DynamoDB stream. Each event has its own structure, so you'll have to write your code accordingly. In this example, we are going to define a custom event format struct CustomEvent, which contains a single field called first_name. The struct implements the Deserialize trait from serde. We also use serde's rename feature to rename the field from firstName (JSON convention) to first_name (Rust convention). Similarly, we define a CustomOutput as the lambda's output format.

The my_handler function is very straightforward; it first checks if the first_name field in the input event is non-empty, otherwise it stops immediately with bail!(). If the first_name is non-empty, it returns a custom output with a message "Hello, <first_name>!".

Besides the event, the handler also receives a Context struct. The Context contains information like the function name, function version, request ID, and much more. The ID is unique for each invocation request, so it's very useful to include it in the log to distinguish the logs from different invocations.

There is one more thing to set up before you can compile the code. You need to install a new compile target x86_64-unknown-linux-musl[4] by running the following:

```
rustup target add x86_64-unknown-linux-musl
```

---

[4]musl is a lightweight C standard library implementation. It allows you to build fully statically-linked binaries.

---

**Note**    If you are cross-compiling on Linux, installing the `musl` target is enough. But if you are compiling on macOS, you also need to install an extra library and to configure the linker using the instructions here: `https://aws.amazon.com/blogs/opensource/rust-runtime-for-aws-lambda/`.

---

Finally, we can compile `src/main.rs` into `./target/x86 64-unknown-linux-musl/release/bootstrap`, then zip it into a ZIP file named `rust.zip`:

```
cargo build --release --target x86_64-unknown-linux-musl
zip -j rust.zip ./target/x86_64-unknown-linux-musl/release/bootstrap
```

To test the lambda, you need to do the following:

1. Visit the AWS Management Console `https://aws.amazon.com/console/` from your browser. Log in with your credentials.

2. In Find Services, find Lambda and click on the result.

3. In the Lambda console (Figure 5-1), click Create Function.

4. In the function creation page, select Author From Scratch. Set the Function Name as `hello-world`. Select Custom Runtime - Provide Your Own Bootstrap on Amazon Linux 2 in the Runtime field. Then click Create Function.

5. Once you are redirected to the `hello-world` function's page, scroll down to the Function Code section and click Actions. Then select the Upload a .zip File option and upload the `rust.zip` file you created previously (Figure 5-2).

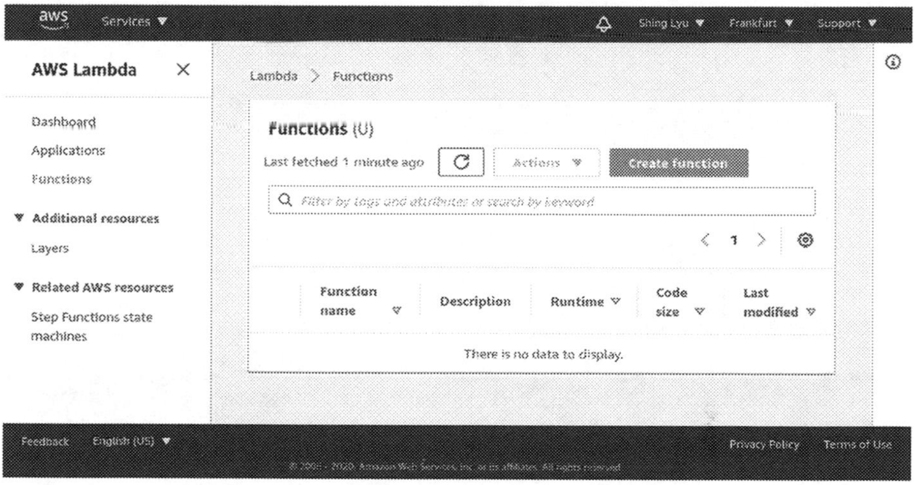


*Figure 5-1. Lambda console*

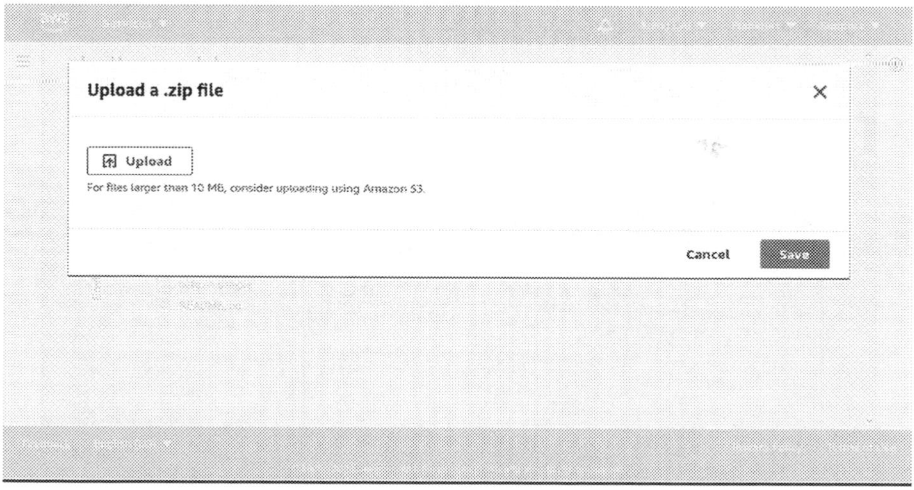


*Figure 5-2. Uploading the zip file*

To test this lambda, you can click on the Test button on the Lambda page (Figure 5-3). If it's the first time you are testing it, AWS console will prompt you to create a test event (Figure 5-4). You can give it an event name called Test add a test event body like so:

```
{
  "firstName": "Shing"
}
```

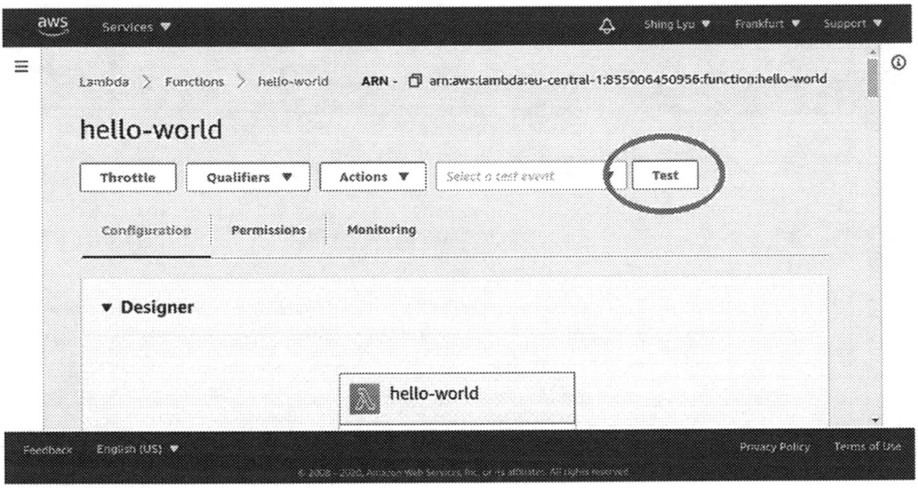

***Figure 5-3.*** *The test button*

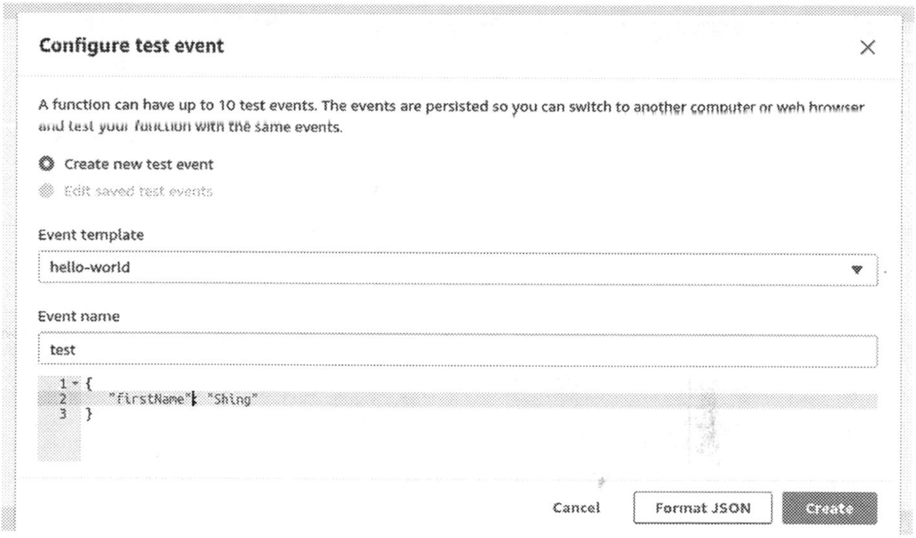

**Figure 5-4.** *Creating a test event*

Then click Create. Now the drop-down menu will show a test event named Test. If you click Test again, the test event will be sent to the lambda and you should see an output and some logs, as shown in Figure 5-5.

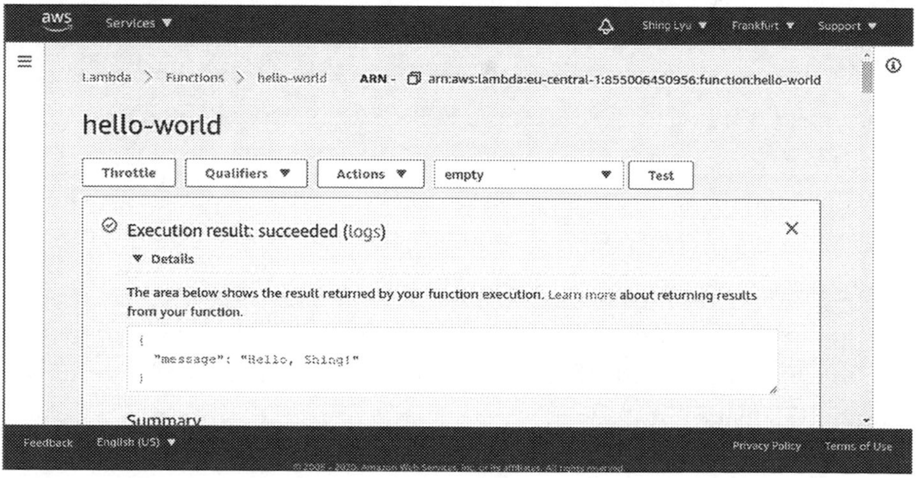

**Figure 5-5.** *Test output*

You can see the lambda is working just as expected.

# Making a REST API with Lambda

The lambda in the previous section can't serve HTTP requests just yet. To be able to receive HTTP requests, we need to put an API Gateway REST API in front of it. The complete architecture would look like Figure 5-6.

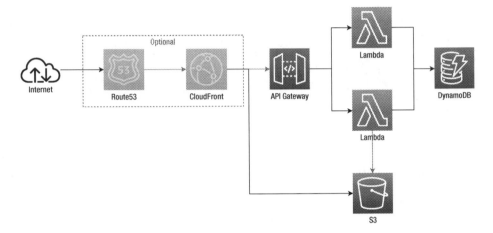

***Figure 5-6.***  *A simple REST API architecture*

The REST APIs are served through API Gateway. API Gateway handles the HTTP connection and triggers a lambda for each request. If we are serving two APIs (e.g., GET /cats and POST /cat), we can have one lambda per API. The database we choose is AWS DynamoDB. DynamoDB is a NoSQL database that is performant and fully managed. We can directly access DynamoDB from the lambdas with the AWS SDK.

We also have a few frontend files: HTML, CSS, and JavaScript. These files can be served separately from an S3 bucket. An S3 bucket is an object store in which we can store files. S3 also has an option to serve your files through HTTP like a static web server.

The URLs exposed by API Gateway and S3 static file hosting are auto-generated by AWS, so you can't really customize them. You can add a CloudFront CDN and add a custom domain name through Route53, a managed DNS service. This way you have full control over what domain name the API and static files use. But this part is beyond the scope of the book and it's not related to Rust, so we'll not show it here. You can consult the official AWS documentation on how to do this.

# Using the Serverless Framework

Configuring all these resources through the web console is not an easy task. It's hard to keep track of what is actually deployed in production. It's also hard to re-create the whole stack from scratch if you destroy it by accident. Infrastructure-as-Code (IaC) is a concept that can solve this problem. You define your infrastructure and the configuration through code, and the IaC tool of your choice will configure everything according to your code. If you make any changes to the definition, the change can also be reflected with a quick deployment. This way, you can version control your infrastructure like code, and fixing or re-creating the whole stack is just a simple deployment away.

Each cloud platform has its IaC service, like AWS CloudFormation, Azure Resource Manager, and Google Cloud Platform Deployment Manager. There are also third-party services that can work cross-platform, like Terraform and Pulumi. In this chapter, we are going to use the Serverless Application Framework, or *Serverless* for short. Serverless not only manages the infrastructure (using AWS CloudFormation under the hood), but it also helps you manage the whole lifecycle of the application like testing, packaging the lambda code, and logging.

We are going to use the prebuilt template `serverless-aws-rust-multi` as the basis for our new serverless catdex. A Serverless framework template contains a Serverless framework configuration and example code to get you started quickly. Because we need to create multiple lambda functions, one for each API, we choose the `serverless-aws-rust-multi`. This template uses cargo workspaces to manage multiple packages in one repository. To use the template, you first need to install the latest version of Node.js and NPM. The npm tool also comes in many different versions. You can use the Node Version Manager (nvm[5]) to easily jump between versions. nvm also has an installation script:

```
curl -o- https://raw.githubusercontent.com/nvm-sh/nvm/v0.35.3/
install.sh | bash
```

Once the script finishes successfully, nvm should add some commands to your shell profile/configuration file (e.g., ~/.bash_profile, ~/.bashrc or ~/.zshrc) so the nvm command becomes available:

```
export NVM_DIR="$([ -z "${XDG_CONFIG_HOME-}" ] && \
  printf %s "${HOME}/.nvm" || \
  printf %s "${XDG_CONFIG_HOME}/nvm")"
[ -s "$NVM_DIR/nvm.sh" ] && . "$NVM_DIR/nvm.sh" # This loads nvm
```

If they are not there, add them yourself and restart your shell.

Once nvm is ready, install the latest Node.js and NPM (I use v13.11.0):

```
nvm install v13.11.0
```

Finally, you can run the following command to use the template to create a new project called serverless-catdex:

```
npx serverless install \
 --url https://github.com/softprops/serverless-aws-rust-multi \
 --name serverless-catdex
```

The npx command comes with npm. It allows you to run a one-off command (in our case, serverless) without installing the package explicitly.

---

[5]https://github.com/nvm-sh/nvm

156

The serverless install command creates a project folder named serverless-catdex. You can cd into the folder and run npm install to install all the dependencies.

At the center of this generated project folder is the serverless.yml file (Listing 5-3). This is the main configuration file for the Serverless framework.

***Listing 5-3.*** The serverless.yml Configuration File

```
# ...
service: serverless-catdex
provider:
  name: aws
  runtime: rust
  memorySize: 128
# you can overwrite defaults here
# stage: dev
# region: us-east-1

# you can add statements to the Lambda function's IAM Role here
# ...

package:
  individually: true

plugins:
  - serverless-rust

functions:
  hello:
    # handler value syntax is '{cargo-package-name}.{bin-name}'
    # or '{cargo-package-name}' for short when you are building a
    # default bin for a given package.
    handler: hello
```

```
# ...

world:
  handler: world
  events:
    - http:
        path: /
        method: get

# you can add CloudFormation resource templates here
#resources:
# ...
```

Most of the field names in the serverless.yml file are self-explanatory. However, there are a few fields we want to highlight:

- provider.region: You can choose a region close to you to reduce network latency. For example, I use eu-central-1 (Frankfurt, Germany).

- plugins: serverless-rust: This allows us to use the Rust runtime for our lambda.

- functions: There are two functions, hello and world, and each is a cargo package in the top-level folder of the same name.

The hello lambda is a free-standing one that has no event trigger configured. The world lambda, on the other hand, receives events from API Gateway, which is specified by the events.http configuration. Also notice that the world lambda uses the lambda_http crate instead of the lambda crate. The lambda_http crate is a specialized crate for building API Gateway event-focused lambdas.

The Serverless framework needs to have access to your AWS account so it can create resources on your behalf. You can follow the step-by-step instructions to set it up at `https://www.serverless.com/framework/docs/providers/aws/guide/credentials/`. To summarize, you need to:

1.  Log in to the AWS console with your root account and go to the Identity & Access Management (IAM) page.

2.  Create a new user with programmatic access. Attach the `AdministratorAccess` policy[6] to it.

3.  Copy the newly-created user's Access Key and Secret Access Key.

Then run the following command to give serverless access:

```
npx serverless config credentials \
  --provider aws \
  --key <YOUR-ACCESS-KEY-HERE> \
  --secret <YOUR-SECRET-ACCESS-KEY-HERE>
```

# Building the /cats API

We are finally ready to build a REST API on AWS lambda and the Serverless framework. We are going to repurpose the `world` lambda to be our `/cats` API. First, let's rename the folder:

```
mv world cats
```

---

[6]It's a bad idea to give your IAM user administrator access in production. You should grant permission based on the principle of least privilege.

Then we need to change the package name in `cats/Cargo.toml`:

```
[package]
name = "cats"
# ...
```

In the root-level folder, we also need to change the `Cargo.toml` file and `serverless.yml`.

```
# Cargo.toml
[workspace]
members = ["hello", "cats"]

# ...
functions:
  hello:
    handler: hello

cats: # Rename this
  handler: cats # And this
  events:
    - http:
        path: /cats # Add this
        method: get
```

We need a database to store the cat's information. We could use Amazon's Relational Database Service (RDS) to run a PostgreSQL database, so we can reuse the same code from the previous chapter. However, in order to show how AWS SDK works, we are going to use DynamoDB, a NoSQL database provided by AWS.

To provision the database, we need to declare it in the `serverless.yml` file, as shown in Listing 5-4.

**Listing 5-4.**  Declaring the DynamoDB in `serverless.yml`

```
service: serverless-catdex
provider:
  name: aws
  runtime: rust
  memorySize: 128
  region: eu-central-1
  iamRoleStatements:
      - Effect: "Allow"
      Action:
          - "dynamodb:Scan"
      Resource:
        Fn::Join:
          - ""
          - - "arn:aws:dynamodb:*:*:table/"
            - "Ref": "CatdexTable"
# ...
functions:
# ...

resources:
  Resources:
    CatdexTable:
      Type: AWS::DynamoDB::Table
      Properties:
        TableName: shing_catdex
        AttributeDefinitions:
            - AttributeName: name
              AttributeType: S
```

```
KeySchema:
    - AttributeName: name
      KeyType: HASH
ProvisionedThroughput:
    ReadCapacityUnits: 1
    WriteCapacityUnits: 1
```

Let's first focus on the resources section. We declared a resource called CatdexTable, which has the Type AWS::DynamoDB::Table. Serverless framework will use CloudFormation, an infrastructure-as-code service, to create the DynamoDB for us. We also defined a few properties of the table, like the name shing_catdex that is used to identify the table in AWS. Due to DynamoDB's design, the data is partitioned into multiple physical storage units. Therefore, you must define a unique *partition key* for each item so they can be partitioned properly. We define an attribute called name and mark it as the partition key using KeySchema. Finally, we provision the desired throughput of the table. Since this is just a demo database, we set both the read and write capacity to 1 to minimize cost.

---

**Note**    CloudFormation is an infrastructure-as-code service. It allows you to declare the AWS resources (i.e., your infrastructure) you need in a JSON or YAML format template. CloudFormation will create, update, or delete the resources on your behalf to match the declared template. This allows you to manage complex infrastructure without having to click hundreds of buttons on the AWS console. You can also utilize all the coding best practices like version control and code review on your infrastructure configuration.

---

By default, the lambda does not have permission to use the DynamoDB. You need to explicitly allow this using AWS Identity and Access Management (IAM). Therefore, in the provider section, we add an iamRoleStatement, which grants the lambda permission to do a dynamodb::Scan operation on the CatdexTable. Now you can run npx serverless deploy and Serverless will create the DynamoDB in your AWS account.

To access the DynamoDB from code, we need to use the Rusoto[7] AWS SDK. Because AWS has over 175 services[8], Rusoto has one crate for each service. So we need to add the rusoto_core and rusoto_dynamodb crates to our cats crate. You can achieve this by:

```
cd cats
cargo add rusoto_core rusoto_dynamodb
```

Once the dependencies are ready, we can finally write the code for cats/src/main.rs, as shown in Listing 5-5.

***Listing 5-5.*** Code for the /cats API

```
use lambda_http::http::{Response, StatusCode};
use lambda_http::{
    handler, lambda, Context, IntoResponse, Request,
};
use rusoto_core::Region;
use rusoto_dynamodb::{DynamoDb, DynamoDbClient, ScanInput};
use serde_json::json;
use std::collections::HashMap;

type Error = Box<dyn std::error::Error + Sync + Send + 'static>;

#[tokio::main]
async fn main() -> Result<(), Error> {
    lambda::run(handler(cats)).await?;
    Ok(())
}
```

---

```rust
async fn cats(
    _: Request,
    _: Context,
) -> Result<impl IntoResponse, Error> {
    let client = DynamoDbClient::new(Region::EuCentral1);

    let scan_input = ScanInput {
        table_name: "shing_catdex".to_string(),
        limit: Some(100),
        ..Default::default()
    };

    let response = match client.scan(scan_input).await {
        Ok(output) => match output.items {
            Some(items) => json!(items
                .into_iter()
                .map(|item| item
                    .into_iter()
                    .map(|(k, v)| (k, v.s.unwrap()))
                    .collect())
                .collect::<Vec<HashMap<String, String>>>())
            .into_response(),
            None => Response::builder()
                .status(StatusCode::NOT_FOUND)
                .body("No cat yet".into())
                .expect("Failed to render response"),
        },
        Err(error) => Response::builder()
            .status(StatusCode::INTERNAL_SERVER_ERROR)
            .body(format!("{:?}", error).into())
            .expect("Failed to render response"),
    };

    Ok(response)
}
```

The `main()` function simply calls `lambda::run(handler(cats))` and awaits on it. The `cats` function is where the magic happens. The first thing we do in the `cats` function is create a `DynamoDBClient` provided by Rusoto.[9] We want to use `client.scan()` to get a list of cats. Because the `scan` operation allows you to filter the results, we need to specify those filtering criteria as a `ScanInput` and pass them to `client.scan()`. Our `ScanInput` specifies the `table_name` we want and the `limit` of 100, so we'll get at most 100 cats. For the other optional fields in `ScanInput`, we simply use the default values.

---

**Note**    DynamoDB supports two major ways for querying data: query and scan. When you query, you need to specify the partition key so DynamoDB can directly find the item. Scan, on the other hand, needs to scan through the whole table. You can specify filtering criteria to further refine the result.

Scan is significantly slower than query, but it's useful for situations when you don't know the partition key in advance. If you already know the partition key you are trying to find, always use query over scan.

---

We then call `client.scan()` and await on the result. We use a `match` block to handle possible errors. If the scan result is an `Err`, then something unexpected has happened. We use the `Response::builder()` to construct a `500 Internal Server Error`.

---

[9]We hard-coded the region to `Region::EuCentral1` to match our configuration in `serverless.yml`. However, if you are deploying the same API in multiple regions for resiliency, you should pass the region by environment variables or other dynamic ways into the lambda.

If the scan returns Ok, then we can see if the output (which has the type ScanOutput) contains anything in its items field. If there is nothing, we return 404 Not Found. If there are some items, we need to convert their format before we return them. The items field has the structure[10]:

```
[
  {
    image_path: {
      s: Some("/image/persian.png")
      // ...
    },
    "name":{
      s: Some("Persian")
      // ...
    }
  }
]
```

With a series of map and collect, we can convert it to:

```
[
  {
    "image_path": "/image/persian.png",
    "name": "Persian"
  }
]
```

Finally, we use json!() to convert it to JSON (serde_json::value::Value). And because the lambda_http crate implements the IntoResponse trait for Value, we can convert it to an HTTP response easily by calling into_response().

---

[10]The s key stands for "string" type.

To test the new API, run `npx serverless deploy`. At the end of the log, you will see the URL for your new API:

```
$ npx scrverless deploy
Serverless: Building Rust hello func...
Serverless: Running containerized build
// ...
Serverless: Packaging service...
Serverless: Creating Stack...
Serverless: Checking Stack create progress...
........
Serverless: Stack create finished...
Serverless: Uploading CloudFormation file to S3...
Serverless: Uploading artifacts...
Serverless: Uploading service hello.zip file to S3 (1001.3
KB)...
Serverless: Validating template...
Serverless: Updating Stack...
Serverless: Checking Stack update progress...
.........................
Serverless: Stack update finished...
Service Information service: serverless-catdex stage: dev
region: eu-central-1
stack: serverless-catdex-dev resources: 10
api keys:
  None
endpoints:
  GET - https://abc0123def.execute-api.eu-central-1.amazonaws.
com/dev/cats
functions:
  hello: serverless-catdex-dev-hello
layers:
  None
```

You can use `curl` to test it:

```
curl https://abc0123def.execute-api.eu-central-1.amazonaws.com/
dev/cats
```

But for now, we don't have any data in the database, so you should see it return an empty object.

# Building the Upload API

Let's build the POST /cat API so we can create a new cat and upload a new image. Since the `hello` lambda is not useful, let's remove the folder (`rm -rf hello`) and remove it from the root-level `Cargo.toml` and `serverless.yml`.

To create a new lambda for the new API, you can simply copy the `cats` API using `cp -r cats cat_post`. Then you need to change or add the name cat_post in a few places:

```
# Root-level Cargo.toml
# Cargo.toml
[workspace]
members = ["cats", "cat_post"]

serverless.yml
# ...
functions:
  cats:
    handler: cats
    events:
    - http:
        path: /cats
        method: get
```

```
cat_post:
  handler: cat_post
  events:
    - http:
        path: /cat
        method: post
# cats_post/Cargo.toml
[package]
name = "cat_post"
# ...
```

In this new API, we need to write data to the DynamoDB, so we need to add the dynamodb:PutItem permission to the IAM role in serverless.yml:

```
provider:
  # ...
  iamRoleStatements:
    - Effect: "Allow"
      Action:
        - "dynamodb:Scan"
        - "dynamodb:PutItem"
      Resource:
        Fn::Join:
          - ""
          - - "arn:aws:dynamodb:*:*:table/"
            - "Ref": "CatdexTable"
```

With the new permission in place, we can write the code in cat_post/src/main.rs (Listing 5-6). The new code uses the serde and serde_json crates for JSON serialization/deserialization, so remember to run cargo add serde serde_json in the cat_post folder.

***Listing 5-6.*** The POST /cat API Code

```rust
use lambda_http::http::{Response, StatusCode};
use lambda_http::{
    handler, lambda, Context, IntoResponse, Request, RequestExt,
};
use rusoto_core::Region;
use rusoto_dynamodb::{
    AttributeValue, DynamoDb, DynamoDbClient, PutItemInput,
};
use serde::Deserialize;
use serde_json::json;
use std::collections::HashMap;

type Error = Box<dyn std::error::Error + Sync + Send + 'static>;

#[derive(Deserialize)]
struct RequestBody {
    name: String,
}

#[tokio::main]
async fn main() -> Result<(), Error> {
    lambda::run(handler(cat_post)).await?;
    Ok(())
}

async fn cat_post(
    request: Request,
    _: Context,
) -> Result<impl IntoResponse, Error> {
    let body: RequestBody = match request.payload() {
        Ok(Some(body)) => body,
```

```rust
    _ => {
        return Ok(Response::builder()
            .status(StatusCode::BAD_REQUEST)
            .body("Invalid payload".into())
            .expect("Failed to render response"))
    }
};

let client = DynamoDbClient::new(Region::EuCentral1);

let mut new_cat = HashMap::new();
new_cat.insert(
    "name".to_string(),
    AttributeValue {
        s: Some(body.name.clone()),
        ..Default::default()
    },
);

let put_item_input = PutItemInput {
    table_name: "shing_catdex".to_string(),
    item: new_cat,
    ..Default::default()
};

match client.put_item(put_item_input).await {
    Ok(_) => (),
    _ => {
        return Ok(Response::builder()
            .status(StatusCode::INTERNAL_SERVER_ERROR)
            .body("Something went wrong when writing to \
                the database".into())
            .expect("Failed to render response"))
    }
}
```

```
    Ok(json!(format!("created cat {}", body.name))
        .into_response())
}
```

The `cat_post()` function does a few things for now:

1.  Extracts the request body (i.e., payload) to get the cat's name.

2.  Creates the DynamoDB client.

3.  Creates a `PutItemInput`, which will create the new cat in the database when passed to `client.put_item()`.

4.  Calls `client.put_item()` to create the DynamoDB item.

In the example in the previous chapter, we uploaded the cat's image through the API. However, API Gateway has a payload size limit of 10MB, so the image needs to be smaller than that. In order to overcome that, we're going to use the S3 presigned URL, which we'll discuss shortly. For now, this example doesn't contain the file upload part.

Notice that the `cat_post()` function now takes an event (the first parameter) of the type `Request`; this is provided by `lambda_http` crate. You can call `request.payload()` to get the request body. We expect the body to have the form:

```
{
  "name": "Persian"
}
```

So we define a `RequestBody` struct, which derives the `serde::Deserialize` trait, to tell Rust how to deserialize it. When we call `request.payload()`, if the return value is a `Some(RequestBody)`, we can assign it to a variable `body`.

Next, we create the DynamoDB client and prepare the `PutItemInput`. The `PutItemInput` expects the table name and a new item (as a `HashMap`). Therefore, we use the cat's name specified in `body` for the new cat's name. For every place that might fail (e.g., parsing payload or calling `put_item()`), we use `match` to handle the errors and return an appropriate HTTP response.

# Uploading the Image Using S3 Presigned URL

As mentioned, API Gateway has a 10MB request size limit, so we can't upload image files larger than that. To overcome this limitation, we can use the S3 presigned PUT URL. You can use the AWS API to upload a file to S3, but since the S3 bucket is private by default, you need to provide valid credentials so AWS can verify your identity and check if you have the proper access to the bucket. However, there is no secure way to store the AWS credentials on the frontend page. A presigned URL can solve this problem. A presigned URL allows anyone to upload files to the predefined S3 location within a limited time, without the need to provide AWS credentials. When creating the presigned URL, you provide AWS credentials, so the user of the URL will get the same permission as the credentials used to sign it. The presigned URL generation takes place in the backend (i.e., in the lambda function), so the credentials are never exposed to the frontend.

In our use case, we can let the frontend call the `POST /cat` endpoint, to create the cat in the DynamoDB. Then, the `POST /cat` API needs to generate a presigned URL and return it to the frontend. Then the frontend uses this presigned URL to upload the cat image directly to S3. Figure 5-7 shows a sequence diagram for this flow. Since this is a demo, the image will then be directly served through the S3 built-in server. But in production, you might want to upload the file to a separate bucket, then sanitize the image, before putting it into the bucket that serves the static files.

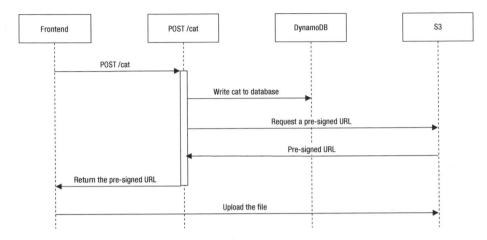

**Figure 5-7.** *Sequence diagram for adding a new cat using the presigned URL*

This approach has a few advantages over uploading through API Gateway and Lambda. First, S3 allows you to upload files up to 5GB[11]. Second, we save bandwidth going through API Gateway, and we also save processing time and memory usage in our lambda, potentially saving some money.

To be able to generate a presigned URL, we need to add the `rusoto_s3` and `rusoto_credentials` crates by running `cargo add rusoto_s3 rusoto_credentials`. Then we need to create an S3 bucket in `serverless.yml`:

```
# ...
resources:
  Resources:
    CatdexTable:
      # ...
```

---

[11]If you use the multipart upload, the limit can be increased to 5TB.

```
FrontendBucket:
  Type: AWS::S3::Bucket
  Properties:
    BucketName: shing-catdex-frontend
    AccessControl: Private
```

---

**Tip**   An S3 bucket name must be globally unique, even across accounts. So you need to choose a different bucket name, e.g., `your-name-catdex-frontend`.

---

Because the presigned URL will get the same permission as the AWS role that creates it, we need to add the `PutObject` permission to our IAM role so the presigned URL can upload files. Change the IAM role in `serverless.yml` like so:

```
iamRoleStatements:
    - Effect: "Allow"
      Action:
          - "dynamodb:Scan"
          - "dynamodb:PutItem"
      Resource:
        Fn::Join:
          - ""
          - - "arn:aws:dynamodb:*:*:table/"
            - "Ref": "CatdexTable"
    - Effect: "Allow"
      Action:
          - "s3:PutObject"
          - "s3:PutObjectAcl"
```

```
Resource:
  Fn::Join:
    - ""
    - - "arn:aws:s3:::"
      - "Ref": "FrontendBucket"
      - "/*"
```

As you can see, we added an `Allow` block that grants `s3:PutObject` and
`s3:PutObjectAcl` permission for everything in the S3 bucket. Let's add
some code to `cat_post/src/main.rs` so we can generate the presigned
URL (Listing 5-7).

***Listing 5-7.*** Generating Presigned URL

```rust
use lambda_http::http::{HeaderValue, Response, StatusCode};
use lambda_http::{
    handler, lambda, Context, IntoResponse, Request, RequestExt,
};
use rusoto_core::Region;
use rusoto_credential::{
    ChainProvider, ProvideAwsCredentials
};
use rusoto_dynamodb::{
    AttributeValue, DynamoDb, DynamoDbClient, PutItemInput,
};
use rusoto_s3::util::PreSignedRequest;
use rusoto_s3::PutObjectRequest;
use serde::Deserialize;
use serde_json::json;
use std::collections::HashMap;

type Error = Box<dyn std::error::Error + Sync + Send + 'static>;
```

```rust
#[derive(Deserialize)]
struct RequestBody {
    name: String,
}

#[tokio::main]
async fn main() -> Result<(), Error> {
    lambda::run(handler(cat_post)).await?;
    Ok(())
}

async fn cat_post(
    request: Request,
    _: Context,
) -> Result<impl IntoResponse, Error> {
    let body: RequestBody = match request.payload() {
        Ok(Some(body)) => body,
        _ => {
            return Ok(
                // ... generate the bad request response
            );
        }
    };

    let client = DynamoDbClient::new(Region::EuCentral1);

    let mut new_cat = HashMap::new();
    new_cat.insert(
        "name".to_string(),
        AttributeValue {
            s: Some(body.name.clone()),
            ..Default::default()
        },
    );
```

```rust
let image_path = format!("image/{}.jpg", &body.name);
new_cat.insert(
    "image_path".to_string(),
    AttributeValue {
        s: Some(image_path.clone()),
        ..Default::default()
    },
);

let put_item_input = PutItemInput {
    table_name: "shing_catdex".to_string(),
    item: new_cat,
    ..Default::default()
};

match client.put_item(put_item_input).await {
    Ok(_) => (),
    _ => {
        return Ok(
            // ... generate internal server error response
        );
    }
}

let credentials =
    ChainProvider::new().credentials().await.unwrap();

let put_request = PutObjectRequest {
    bucket: "shing-catdex-frontend".to_string(),
    key: image_path,
    content_type: Some("image/jpeg".to_string()),
    ..Default::default()
};
```

```
let presigned_url = put_request.get_presigned_url(
    &Region::EuCentral1,
    &credentials,
    &Default::default(),
);

let mut response =
    json!({ "upload_url": presigned_url }).into_response();
Ok(response)
}
```

The first thing we did is added an image_path to the new_cat that will be inserted into the database. The image_path is hard-coded to be the image/<cat_name>.jpg.[12] When we generate the presigned URL later, the name will be fixed, so no matter what file the user uploads, it will be renamed as image/<cat_name>.jpg in S3.

To create the presigned URL, we need to create a PutObjectRequest first. The PutObjectRequest represents an attempt to upload a file to S3. We can get the presigned URL by calling .get_presigned_url() on the PutObjectRequest. We need to provide AWS credentials to .get_presigned_url(). Whoever uses this URL will get the same permission as the credentials that were used to sign it. Therefore, we get the lambda's execution role credentials using the rusoto_credentials::ChainProvider. Using these credentials, the user will get the s3::PutObject permission we defined in the serverless.yml file. We then add the URL to the response body so the frontend can receive it.

---

[12]We could also support more file extensions (e.g., .png or .bmp). But for simplicity, we allow users only to upload JPEG files.

> **Note**    The `ChainProvider` will try to find the AWS credentials
> from multiple sources using a priority order. For example, by looking
> for the `AWS_ACCESS_KEY_ID` and `AWS_SECRET_ACCESS_KEY_ID`
> environment variables, or the AWS credentials file, or the IAM
> instance profile in EC2. The lambda runtime will provide the
> `AWS_ACCESS_KEY_ID` and `AWS_SECRET_ACCESS_KEY` environment
> variables (for the lambda's execution role) to the lambda by default,
> so the `ChainProvider` can get the credentials.

You can deploy to AWS with `npx serverless deploy`. If you call
the API with `curl`, you should receive the presigned URL in the
response body:

```
$ curl --header "Content-Type: application/json" \
  --request POST \
  --data '{"name": "Persian"}' \
  https://abc0123def.execute-api.eu-central-1.amazonaws.com/
  dev/cat

{

  "upload_url":"https://s3.eu-central-1.amazonaws.com/shing-
  catdex-frontend/image/Persian.jpg?X-Amz-Algorithm=AWS4-HMAC-
  SHA256&X-Amz-credentials=...&X-Amz-Date=20200819T095109Z&X-
  Amz-Expires=3600&X-Amz-Security-Token=...&X-Amz-Signature
  =...&X-Amz-SignedHeaders=host"
}
```

You can use this URL to upload the file like so:

```
$ curl -X PUT -T persian.jpg -L -v "https://s3.eu-central-1.
amazonaws.com/shing-catdex-frontend/image/Persian.jpg?X
Amz-Algorithm=AWS4-HMAC-SHA256&X-Amz-credentials=...&X-Amz-
Date=20200819T095109Z&X-Amz-Expires=3600&X-Amz-Security-
Token=...&X-Amz-Signature=...&X-Amz-SignedHeaders=host"
```

This uploads a file on the local machine named `persian.jpg`. A few fields, like `X-Amz-credentials` and `Amx-Security-Token`, are omitted because they change every time you generate a new URL.

# Adding the Frontend

Now with the API ready, we can also serve the HTML, JavaScript, and CSS on AWS. We can upload the files to an S3 bucket and enable "static website hosting" on that S3 bucket. To automate this process, we will use the `serverless-finch` plugin. Such a plugin uploads the files for us and makes all the necessary configurations to enable static website hosting.

To install this plugin, run `npm install --save serverless-finch`. After installing the plugin, modify `serverless.yml` to Listing 5-8 so the plugin will use the `shing-catdex-frontend` S3 bucket we created before to serve the static files.

***Listing 5-8.*** Using the `serverless-finch` Plugin

```
# ...
plugins:
  - serverless-rust
  - serverless-finch

resources:
  Resources:
    # ...
    FrontendBucket:
      Type: AWS::S3::Bucket
```

```
    Properties:
      BucketName: shing-catdex-frontend # Change this to
      your-name-catdex-frontend
      AccessControl: Private
custom:
  client:
    bucketName: shing-catdex-frontend
```

By default, the serverless-finch plugin looks for files in the client/dist folder and uploads them to S3. So we need to create the folder using mkdir -p client/dist. Then create the following files in it:

- index.html: The cats overview page (Listing 5-9)

- css/index.css: CSS stylesheet for index.html (Listing 5-10)

- add.html: The add new cat form (Listing 5-11)

***Listing 5-9.*** The client/dist/index.html File

```html
<!DOCTYPE html>
<html>
  <head>
    <meta charset="UTF-8" />
    <title>Catdex</title>
    <link rel="stylesheet" href="css/index.css" type="text/css">
  </head>
  <body>
    <h1>Catdex</h1>
    <p>
      <a href="/add.html">Add a new cat</a>
    </p>
```

```html
<section class="cats" id="cats">
  <p>No cats yet</p>
</section>
<script charset="utf-8">
  document.addEventListener("DOMContentLoaded", () => {
    fetch('https://abc0123def.execute-api.eu-central-1.
    amazonaws.com/dev/cats')
      .then((response) => response.json())
      .then((cats) => {
        document.getElementById("cats").innerText = ""
        // Clear the "No cats yet"
        for (cat of cats) {
          const catElement = document.
          createElement("article")
          catElement.classList.add("cat")
          const catTitle = document.createElement("h3")
          const catLink = document.createElement("a")
          catLink.innerText = cat.name
          catLink.href = '/cat.html?id=${cat.id}'
          const catImage = document.createElement("img")
          catImage.src = cat.image_path

          catTitle.appendChild(catLink)
          catElement.appendChild(catTitle)
          catElement.appendChild(catImage)

          document.getElementById("cats").
          appendChild(catElement)
        }
      })
```

```
    })
  </script>
 </body>
</html>
```

*Listing 5-10.* The client/dist/css/index.css File

```css
.cats {
    display: flex;
}

.cat {
  border: 1px solid grey;
  min-width: 200px;
  min-height:  350px;
  margin: 5px;
  padding: 5px;
  text-align: center;
}
.cat > img {
  width: 190px;
}
```

*Listing 5-11.* The client/dist/add.html File

```html
<!DOCTYPE html>
<html>
  <head>
    <meta charset="UTF-8" />
    <title>Catdex</title>
    <link rel="stylesheet" href="static/css/index.css"
     type="text/css">
  </head>
```

```
<body>
  <script>
    async function submitForm(e) {
      e.preventDefault()

      const cat_name = document.getElementById('name').value

      const cat_post_response = await fetch(
        'https://abc0123def.execute-api.eu-central-1.
            amazonaws.com/dev/cat',
        {
          method: 'POST',
          mode: 'cors',
          headers: {
            'Content-Type': 'application/json'
          },
          body: JSON.stringify({ name: cat_name })
        }
      )

      const image_upload_url =
        (await cat_post_response.json()).upload_url

      const image = document.getElementById("image").files[0]

      const image_upload_response = await fetch(
        image_upload_url,
        {
          method: 'PUT',
          body: image,
        }
      )
```

```
        if (image_upload_response.status === 200) {
          alert("Success")
        } else {
          alert("Failed")
        }
        return false
      }
    </script>
    <h1>Add a new cat</h1>

    <form onsubmit="return submitForm(event)">
      <label for="name">Name:</label>
      <input type="text" name="name" id="name" value="" />
      <label for="image">Image:</label>
      <input type="file" name="image" id="image" value="" />
      <button type="submit">Submit</button>
    </form>

  </body>
</html>
```

The index.html and index.css files are mostly the same as the one in the previous chapters. The add.html file has a slightly different logic than before. Instead of just calling the POST /cat API, we also make a second PUT call to update the image.

You can now run npx serverless client deploy to upload these static files to S3. Once it's deployed, you should see the URL in the log output:

```
$ npx serverless client deploy
Serverless: This deployment will:
Serverless: - Upload all files from 'client/dist' to bucket
'shing-catdex-frontend'
# ...
```

```
Serverless: Success! Your site should be available at
  http://shing-catdex-frontend.s3-website.eu-central-1.
  amazonaws.com/
```

However, if you open the website now, you'll notice that the API calls are failing. This is because of the same-origin policy. Under that policy, our web page cannot access APIs under a different origin, which is the combination of URI scheme, hostname, and port. Because the web page is served under `http://shing-catdex-frontend.s3-website.eu-central-1.amazonaws.com/`, but the API is under `https://abc0123def.execute-api.eu-central-1.amazonaws.com/`, the same-origin policy will block the API call. The same-origin policy is a security feature that can block many kinds of attacks.

Since we control both the frontend and the backend API, we can use cross-origin resource sharing (CORS) to overcome this restriction. With CORS enabled on our backend API, it can grant access to the frontend serving from a different origin.

To enable CORS, first we need to add `cors: true` to all the API endpoints in `serverless.yml`:

```
# ...
functions:
  cats:
    handler: cats
    events:
      - http:
          path: /cats
          method: get
          cors: true
  cat_post:
    handler: cat_post
    events:
```

```
        - http:
            path: /cat
            method: post
            cors: true
```

Second, both APIs need to respond with an `Access-Control-Allow-Origin` header. This header specifies the origin that is allowed to access it. For simplicity, we specify `Access-Control-Allow-Origin: *`, which allows every origin. This is of course not very secure. If you are running production workloads, always explicitly specify the exact host.

To add this header to the API, we can tweak the `cats/src/main.rs` file, as shown in Listing 5-12.

***Listing 5-12.***  Adding CORS Header to Cats GET API

```rust
use lambda_http::http::{HeaderValue, Response, StatusCode};
// ...

#[tokio::main]
async fn main() -> Result<(), Error> {
    lambda::run(handler(cats)).await?;
    Ok(())
}

async fn cats(
    _: Request,
    _: Context,
) -> Result<impl IntoResponse, Error> {
    // ...

    let mut response = match client.scan(scan_input).await {
        // ...
    };

    response.headers_mut().insert(
        "Access-Control-Allow-Origin",
```

```
        HeaderValue::from_static("*"),
    );

    Ok(response)
}
```

Make a similar change to `cat_post/src/main.rs`, as shown in Listing 5-13.

***Listing 5-13.*** Adding CORS Header to Cat POST API

```rust
use lambda_http::http::{HeaderValue, Response, StatusCode};
// ...

#[tokio::main]
async fn main() -> Result<(), Error> {
    lambda::run(handler(cat_post)).await?;
    Ok(())
}

async fn cat_post(
    request: Request,
    _: Context,
) -> Result<impl IntoResponse, Error> {
    // ...
    let mut response =
        json!({ "upload_url": presigned_url }).into_response();

    response.headers_mut().insert(
        "Access-Control-Allow-Origin",
        HeaderValue::from_static("*"),
    );

    Ok(response)
}
```

Finally, there is a small issue with the default CORS setting set by
serverless-finch. It allows PUT requests from https://*.amazonaws.com,
but our frontend is served using HTTP, not HTTPS. Therefore, you need to
manually reconfigure the CORS setting using the AWS console:

1. Open the AWS console.

2. Go to S3.

3. Click on the shing-catdex-frontend bucket.

4. Go to the Permissions tab, then click CORS
   Configuration.

5. Change https://*.amazonaws.com to
   http://*.amazonaws.com (Listing 5-14).

***Listing 5-14.*** The CORS Configuration for S3

```xml
<?xml version="1.0" encoding="UTF-8"?>
<CORSConfiguration xmlns="http://s3.amazonaws.com/doc/2006-03-01/">
<CORSRule>
    <AllowedOrigin>http://*.amazonaws.com</AllowedOrigin>
    <AllowedMethod>PUT</AllowedMethod>
    <AllowedMethod>POST</AllowedMethod>
    <AllowedMethod>DELETE</AllowedMethod>
    <MaxAgeSeconds>0</MaxAgeSeconds>
    <AllowedHeader>*</AllowedHeader>
</CORSRule>
<CORSRule>
    <AllowedOrigin>*</AllowedOrigin>
    <AllowedMethod>GET</AllowedMethod>
    <MaxAgeSeconds>0</MaxAgeSeconds>
    <AllowedHeader>*</AllowedHeader>
</CORSRule>
</CORSConfiguration>
```

Because `serverless-finch` will override your CORS configuration by default, you need to deploy it with an extra flag, called `--no-cors-change`. Also, `serverless-finch` will remove all the files in the bucket during deployment, so all the uploaded cat images will be lost. You can use the `--no-delete-contents` flag to tell `serverless-finch` to keep the files. Therefore, the command to deploy the frontend now becomes:

```
npx serverless client deploy --no-delete-contents --no-cors-
change
```

Now if you run the `npx serverless deploy` and `npx serverless client deploy --no-delete-con--no-cors-change` commands, the catdex website should work just like the one in the previous chapters.

# Other Alternatives

Of the top three cloud providers (AWS, Google Cloud Platform, and Microsoft Azure), only AWS has experimental support for Rust, as we've introduced in this chapter. There is an unofficial, community-driven Azure SDK for Rust.[13] And there have been attempts to run Rust in Azure Function[14], but they are also unofficial.

---

[13]`https://github.com/Azure/azure-sdk-for-rust`
[14]`https://robertohuertas.com/2018/12/22/azure-function-rust/`

# CHAPTER 6

# High-Performance Web Frontend Using WebAssembly

We've seen how Rust can help us in the backend in many different ways: static web servers, REST APIs, serverless computing, and WebSocket. But can you use Rust in the frontend? The answer is yes! With the introduction of *WebAssembly*[1] (abbreviated *Wasm*), you can compile a Rust program to WebAssembly and run it in browsers, alongside JavaScript.

## What Is WebAssembly?

WebAssembly is an open standard for a binary instruction format that runs on a stack-based virtual machine. Its original design goal was to provide near-native performance in web browsers. You can think of it as an assembly language for the web. WebAssembly is a World Wide Web Consortium (W3C) recommendation, and it's implemented in all major browsers.

WebAssembly is designed to run at near-native speed. It doesn't require you to use a garbage collector (GC).[2] It can be a compile target for

---

[1]https://webassembly.org/

[2]There are discussions underway to add GC as an optional feature.

© Shing Lyu 2021
S. Lyu, *Practical Rust Web Projects*, https://doi.org/10.1007/978-1-4842-6589-5_6

many languages, like C, C++, and Rust. Therefore, you can write frontend applications in the high-level programming language you prefer and get predictable performance.

There are a few reasons that you might want to use Rust to compile to WebAssembly:

- To enjoy the high-level syntax and low-level control of Rust in browsers

- To save bandwidth while downloading the small `.wasm` binary because of Rust's minimal runtime

- To reuse the extensive collection of existing Rust libraries

- To use familiar frontend tools, like ES6 modules, `npm`, and `webpack`, through the `wasm-pack` toolchain

There are also some common misconceptions about WebAssembly:

- WebAssembly does not replace JavaScript completely. It is supposed to run alongside JavaScript and complement it.

- WebAssembly is not limited to the browsers, although it initially targeted the browser. The WebAssembly runtime can potentially run anywhere. For example, on the server side or in IoT devices.

A common use case for WebAssembly is to speed up the performance bottleneck of JavaScript web applications. The user interface (UI) can be built in HTML, CSS, and JavaScript. But when the application needs to execute CPU-intensive jobs, it calls WebAssembly. The result of the computation can then be passed back to JavaScript for display.

Some framework takes this idea further to let you write the whole frontend application in Rust. They usually take inspiration from other popular frontend frameworks like React and Elm and use a Virtual DOM[3]. The Rust code is compiled to Wasm and rendered to the screen by the Virtual DOM.

# What Are You Building?

First, you'll be building a Hello World application. This application will create a browser `alert()` from Rust. This example will show you the process of getting a WebAssembly program up and running. You'll also learn how WebAssembly works with JavaScript.

In the Catdex example from Chapter 2, you allow users to upload cat photos. But the user might upload a very high-resolution photo that takes a lot of bandwidth. To save bandwidth, you can resize the photo in the frontend before uploading it. But image resizing is a CPU-intensive job, so it makes sense to implement the resize algorithm in WebAssembly. You'll be building a frontend application to reduce the size of a cat image.

Once you understand how WebAssembly can work with JavaScript, you can start to use a fully Rust frontend framework. You'll first start with a hello world-style example to get familiar with the setup and build process. This example will have a button that increases a counter.

Finally, you'll be rebuilding the cat photo resize application with the Yew[4] framework.

---

[3]https://reactjs.org/docs/faq-internals.html#what-is-the-virtual-dom
[4]https://yew.rs

# Hello WebAssembly!

There are quite a few steps to run a Hello World program in WebAssembly. Conceptually, this is how you get some Rust code running in the browser as WebAssembly:

1.  Write the Rust code to expose functionality to JavaScript and to handle data passing between JavaScript and Wasm.

2.  Use the compiler toolchain to compile Rust code into a `.wasm` binary.

3.  Serve the `.wasm` file on a web server.

4.  Write an HTML and JavaScript page to load this `.wasm` file.

5.  In the JavaScript file, `fetch`[5] the `.wasm` file and use the `WebAssembly.instantiateStreaming()`[6] API to compile and instantiate the `.wasm` module.

6.  In JavaScript, make calls to the functions that the `.wasm` module exports.

These steps are tedious and do not feel as ergonomic as what `cargo` or `npm` offer. Thankfully, there is a tool called `wasm-pack` that bundles many tools that make this process smoother. Also, to avoid writing boilerplate code, you can use the `wasm-pack-template`[7] template to quickly generate a project.

---

[5]Fetch is a web API that allows you to download additional resources. It's a successor of the old `XMLHttpRequest`.

[6]Check `https://developer.mozilla.org/en-US/docs/WebAssembly/Loading_and_running` for more detail.

[7]`https://github.com/rustwasm/wasm-pack-template`

# Setting Up the Development Environment

To set up `wasm-pack`, head to `https://rustwasm.github.io/wasm-pack/installer/`. For Linux, it's as simple as executing the following command in the terminal[8]:

```
curl https://rustwasm.github.io/wasm-pack/installer/init.sh \
    -sSf | sh
```

`Wasm-pack` helps you package the project into an npm (Node Package Manager) package, so developers who are familiar with modern JavaScript development can easily pick it up. To properly package and publish the package, you need to install the command-line `npm` the same way as in Chapter 5.

Finally, we need to install `cargo-generate`, a `cargo` subcommand that helps you create new projects using templates. Simply run this command in the command line:

```
cargo install cargo-generate
```

# Creating the Project

Now you have all the required tools installed. You can start creating the project by running:

```
cargo generate --git https://github.com/rustwasm/wasm-pack-template
```

This command makes `cargo-generate` download the `wasm-pack-template` template from GitHub and create a project locally. `Cargo-generate` will ask you for the project name; you can name it `hello-wasm`. After `cargo-generate` finishes, you'll see a `hello-wasm` folder in the current directory.

---

[8]`curl` is a popular command-line HTTP client. If you don't have it, you can almost certainly find it in your Linux distribution's package directory.

In the hello-wasm folder, you'll find a fairly typical cargo library project, with Cargo.toml and src/lib.rs. But if you look closely into the Cargo.toml file shown in Listing 6-1, you'll see it has a few interesting features.[9]

***Listing 6-1.*** Cargo.toml Generated by cargo-generate

```
[package]
name = "hello-wasm"
version = "0.1.0"
authors = ["Shing Lyu"]
edition = "2018"

[lib]
crate-type = ["cdylib", "rlib"]

[features]
default = ["console_error_panic_hook"]

[dependencies]
wasm-bindgen = "0.2.63"

# The console_error_panic_hook crate provides
# better debugging of panics by logging them with
# console.error. This is great for development,
# but requires all the std::fmt and std::panicking
# infrastructure, so isn't great for code size when deploying.
console_error_panic_hook = {
    version = "0.1.6",
    optional = true
}
```

---

[9]The wasm-pack-template is being updated from time to time. The versions of the dependencies might be newer than the ones listed here.

```
# wee_alloc is a tiny allocator for wasm that is only ~1K
# in code size compared to the default allocator's ~10K.
# It is slower than the default allocator, however.
# Unfortunately, wee_alloc requires nightly Rust when targeting
# wasm for now.
wee_alloc = { version = "0.4.5", optional = true }

[dev-dependencies]
wasm-bindgen-test = "0.3.13"

[profile.release]
# Tell rustc to optimize for small code size.
opt-level = "s"
```

The crate-type is cdylib (C Dynamic Library) and rlib (Rust Library). Cdylib ensures that the output is a dynamic library that follows the C FFI convention. All the Rust-specific information is stripped away. This will help the LLVM compiler that compiles our code to Wasm understand the exported interfaces. Rlib is added to run unit tests; it's not required to compile to WebAssembly.

Since the browsers will download the .wasm binary through the Internet, it's crucial to keep the binary size small, so the download is fast. You'll notice that in [profile.release], the opt-level option is set to s, which means optimize for small code size. The template also chooses to use a custom memory allocator called wee_alloc that is optimized for code size.

It also adds the wasm-bindgen crate, which is used to generate binding between WebAssembly and JavaScript. You can see the wasm-bindgen crate being used in the src/lib.rs file (Listing 6-2).

*Listing 6-2.* The `lib.rs` File Generated by the Template

```rust
mod utils;

use wasm_bindgen::prelude::*;

// When the wee_alloc feature is enabled, use wee_alloc
// as the global allocator.
#[cfg(feature = "wee_alloc")]
#[global_allocator]
static ALLOC: wee_alloc::WeeAlloc = wee_alloc::WeeAlloc::INIT;

#[wasm_bindgen]
extern {
    fn alert(s: &str);
}

#[wasm_bindgen]
pub fn greet() {
    alert("Hello, hello-wasm!");
}
```

The first few lines in `src/lib.rs` set up the `wee_alloc` allocator, and we won't go into detail about them. The next two blocks are the key in this hello world example. What this file is trying to do is the following:

1. Expose the JavaScript DOM API `window.alert()` to Rust/Wasm.

2. Expose a Wasm function named `greet()` to JavaScript.

3. When JavaScript calls the `greet()` Wasm function, call the `alert()` function from Wasm to display a popup message in the browser.

The following block in Listing 6-2 exposes the window.alert() function to Wasm:

```
#[wasm_bindgen]
extern {
    fn alert(s: &str);
}
```

The extern block tells Rust this function is defined as a foreign function interface (FFI). Rust can call this foreign JavaScript function defined elsewhere.

Notice that the alert function takes a &str. This matches the JavaScript alert, which takes a JS String.

However, in Wasm's specification, you are only allowed to pass integers and floating-point numbers across JavaScript and Wasm. So how can we pass a &str as the parameter? This is the magic of wasm_bindgen. The #[wasm_bindgen] attribute tells wasm_bindgen to create a binding. Wasm_bindgen generates Wasm code that encodes the &str into an integer array, passes it to JavaScript, then generates JavaScript code that converts the integer array back into a JavaScript string.

Wasm_bindgen works the other way around: you can expose a Rust function using pub fn greet() and annotate it with the #[wasm_bindgen] attribute. Wasm_bindgen will compile this function to Wasm and expose it to JavaScript.

---

**Note**    You might be wondering what the src/utils.rs and the console_error_panic_hook feature defined in Cargo.toml do. When Rust code panics, you'll only see a generic Wasm error message in the browser's console. The console_error_panic_hook feature prints a more informative error message about the panic to the browser's console, which helps you with debugging. The console_error_panic_hook feature needs to be explicitly initialized once, and so the src/utils.rs provides a small function to do that.

---

If you now run `wasm-pack build`, `wasm-pack` will ensure that you have the correct toolchain (for example, download the correct compilation target with rustup) and compile your code to Wasm. You'll see the output in the pkg folder. `Wasm-pack` generates a few files:

- `hello_wasm_bg.wasm`: The compiled Wasm binary containing the Rust function you exposed.

- `hello_wasm.js`: Some JavaScript binding wrapper around the Wasm functions that makes passing values easier.

- `hello_wasm_bg.d.ts`: TypeScript type definition. Useful if you want to develop the frontend in TypeScript.

- `hello_wasm.d.ts`: TypeScript definition.

- `package.json`: The npm project metadata file. This will be useful when you publish the package to npm.

- `README.md`: A short introductory note to the package user. It will be shown on the npm website if you publish this package.

---

**Note**    TypeScript is a programming language that builds on JavaScript by adding static type definitions. As a Rust developer, you already know the power of static types. Since the Rust code you write for Wasm is typed, it makes sense to use it with typed TypeScript instead of JavaScript so that you can enjoy the power of static typing end-to-end.

Wasm-pack doesn't force you to use TypeScript, so it generates a .js file containing the implementation and a .d.ts definition file that contains TypeScript type definitions. If the frontend uses JavaScript, it can use the .js file only and ignore the .d.ts file. But if the frontend uses TypeScript, it can reference the .d.ts file to enforce the types.

Because TypeScript is a topic that deserves its own book, I'll stick with JavaScript in this book.

## Creating the Frontend

We have the Wasm package ready, but how do you make it work on a web page? Since Wasm does not support the ES6 import statement yet, you'll have to perform a fetch to download the .wasm file, then call the WebAssembly.instantiateStreaming() web API to instantiate it. This is quite cumbersome and doesn't feel natural to the npm-style workflow. Instead, we can use Webpack to simplify the way we import the Wasm package into a JavaScript application.

Webpack is a versatile tool for bundling your JavaScript files. It can analyze the dependency of your various JavaScript files and packages installed from npm and package them into a single .js file. This reduces the overhead of downloading multiple JavaScript files, and reduces the risk of missing dependencies in runtime. The most important feature we want from Webpack is using the ES6 import statement to import a Wasm package. This allows you to avoid all the boilerplate code of fetching the .wasm file and instantiating it.

Webpack requires some configuration to work with Wasm. To save you this trouble, we are going to use another template, create-wasm-app[10]. This template creates a frontend web page project with Webpack configuration for Wasm. To initiate a project based on this template, simply run the following command in the command-line inside the hello-wasm folder:

```
npm init wasm-app client
```

This command will download the create-wasm-app template[11] and create the project in a folder called client.

---

**Tip**   When you run cargo generate, cargo will initialize a Git project in the created project directory. When you run npm init wasm-app client, npm will also initialize a separate Git repository inside the client folder. So you end up with two Git repositories, one inside the other. If you want to version-control the whole project in one Git repository, you can delete the inner client/.git folder.

---

Since this template creates a frontend project, there should be an HTML file as the entry point. You can find the index.html file in the client folder, shown in Listing 6-3.

*Listing 6-3.*  The index.html File Generated by the Template

```html
<!DOCTYPE html>
<html>
  <head>
    <meta charset="utf-8">
```

---

[10]https://github.com/rustwasm/create-wasm-app

[11]An npm template, officially called an *initializer*, is an npm package with the prefix create- in the name. The command npm init foo is shorthand for npm init create-foo. npm will look for the npm package named create-foo.

```
<title>Hello wasm-pack!</title>
</head>
<body>
  <noscript>
    This page contains webassembly and javascript content,
    please enable javascript in your browser.
  </noscript>
  <script src="./bootstrap.js"></script>
</body>
</html>
```

The index.html file is a very minimal HTML page. It includes the bootstrap.js file, shown in Listing 6-4 with a <script> tag.

***Listing 6-4.*** The bootstrap.js File

```
// A dependency graph that contains any wasm must
// all be imported asynchronously. This 'bootstrap.js'
// file does the single async import, so that no one
// else needs to worry about it again.
import("./index.js")
  .catch(e => console.error("Error importing 'index.js':", e));
```

This bootstrap.js file imports the index.js file asynchronously. This is the limitation of Webpack v4, such that the file cannot be imported synchronously. The index.js file shown in Listing 6-5 is what actually uses the Wasm package.

***Listing 6-5.*** The index.js File

```
import * as wasm from "hello-wasm-pack";

wasm.greet();
```

In index.js, the template imports a demo Wasm package on npm called hello-wasm-pack. But we want to use the Wasm project you just built in the parent directly. How do you change that? You'll need to open the package. json file and add a dependencies section, as shown in Listing 6-6.

***Listing 6-6.*** Adding the Local Dependency in package.json

```
{
  "name": "create-wasm-app",
  // ...
  "dependencies": {
    "hello-wasm": "file:../pkg"
  },
  "devDependencies": {
    // Removed the hello-wasm-pack package
    "webpack": "^4.29.3",
    "webpack-cli": "^3.1.0",
    "webpack-dev-server": "^3.1.5",
    "copy-webpack-plugin": "^5.0.0"
  }
}
```

In dependencies, you defined a new package called hello-wasm, and the file:../pkg means the package is located in the same file system, in the ../pkg folder. Don't forget to remove the unused hello-wasm-pack demo package from devDependencies as well.

Then you can go back to Listing 6-3 and change the first line to this:

```
import * as wasm from "hello-wasm";
```

This will load the hello-wasm package. The next line calls the greet function you exported from Rust:

```
wasm.greet();
```

As mentioned, the `import` statement won't work without Webpack. This template already has all the Webpack configuration we have, including:

- `webpack.config.js`: Webpack-specific configurations.

- `package.json`

  - `devDependencies`: This section specifies all the dependencies like `webpack`, `webpack-cli`, `webpack-dev-serve`, and `copy-webpack-plugin`.

  - `scripts`: This section provides two commands:

    * `build`: Uses Webpack to bundle the source code into the `./dist`[12] folder.

    * `start`: Starts a development server that will bundle the code and serve it right away. It also monitors source code changes and rebundles if needed.

You need to install Webpack and its dependencies by going into the `client` folder and running `npm install`. Once the dependencies are installed, you can run `npm run start`, which will call `webpack-dev-server`. This development server runs Webpack to bundle your code whenever your code changes, and it serves it on the address `http://localhost:8080`. When you open that URL in a web browser, you should see an alert pop up with the message `Hello, hello-wasm!` (Figure 6-1).

---

[12]This is the default location, so you won't find that mentioned in the code or configuration.

*Figure 6-1.* *The popup alert*

The development server, as the name suggests, is for development only. If you want to put this website into production, you'll have to:

- Run `npm run build`.

- Deploy the files created in the `./dist` folder to a production-ready web server.

# Resizing Images with WebAssembly

The hello world project you just implemented might seem trivial. Why should JavaScript call Wasm, then let Wasm call the JavaScript web API `alert`, instead of letting JavaScript call `alert` directly? Where Wasm truly shines is when it replaces the performance bottleneck in JavaScript applications. Because Wasm is designed to run at near-native speed, it makes sense to offload performance-critical parts of a JavaScript application to Wasm, while keeping the rest in JavaScript for flexibility and ease of development.

One example of a performance-critical job is image processing in the frontend. Image-processing algorithms are usually computationally intensive. If one can use Wasm to handle the core image-processing algorithm, it might be able to run much faster than a JavaScript implementation.

You've implemented the cat photo upload service, but it wouldn't be complete without some basic image-processing functionality, like resizing and rotation. Therefore, you're going to build a very basic image processing tool using JavaScript and Wasm. Let's start with one of the simplest functionalities: resizing.

The simplest way to represent an image on a computer is to store the color value of each pixel. As you might have learned in basic physics class, different colors can be created by adding red, green, and blue together at different intensities. If we represent each color component's intensity with an 8-bit integer, we can represent $2^8 \times 2^8 \times 2^8 = 256 \times 256 \times 256 = 1677216$ different colors.

To save storage space, an image can be compressed in many ways so it can be represented more efficiently in memory. There are also hundreds of file formats for storing the image data, like PNG, JPEG, and GIF. Since this is not a book on digital image processing, we are going to rely on an existing Rust crate called `image` to handle all the nitty-gritty of image formats. The `image` crate not only helps you read and write various image formats, it also provides several image-processing algorithms like resize, rotate, invert, etc. This also demonstrates one of the benefits of compiling Rust to Wasm: you can build reliable and high-performance libraries on top of Rust's vibrant crates ecosystem.

First, you need to create a Wasm project using the same command as before:

```
cargo generate --git https://github.com/rustwasm/wasm-pack-template
```

This time, name the project `wasm-image-processing`. Then add the `image` crate to the [dependencies] section in `Cargo.toml`:

```
[package]
name = "wasm-image-processing"
//...
```

```
[dependencies]
wasm-bindgen = "0.2"
image = "0.23.2"
```

Let's think about how the API exposing the JavaScript should look. The first feature we want to expose to JavaScript is a function that can resize an image. To make it easier, we can make the function shrink the image by half, so you don't have to deal with passing different resize ratios. The function might be something like Listing 6-7.

*Listing 6-7.* Wasm API for Shrinking the Image in Half

```rust
extern crate web_sys;

mod utils;

use wasm_bindgen::prelude::*;

// When the wee_alloc feature is enabled, use wee_alloc
// as the global allocator.
#[cfg(feature = "wee_alloc")]
#[global_allocator]
static ALLOC: wee_alloc::WeeAlloc = wee_alloc::WeeAlloc::INIT;
#[wasm_bindgen]
pub fn shrink_by_half(
    original_image: SomeKindOfImageType,
    width: u32,
    height: u32
) -> SomeKindOfImageType {
    // ...
}
```

The shrink_by_half() function should take an image of some type we don't know yet (SomeKindOfImageType), determine the width and height[13] of that image (as u32), and return a smaller image by half.

What type should the original_image and the image it returns be? We can take a hint from the resize function we'll be using from the image crate. The function is located in image::imageops and its function signature is shown in Listing 6-8.[14]

***Listing 6-8.*** Function Signature for image::imageops::resize

```
pub fn resize<I: GenericImageView>(
    image: &I,
    nwidth: u32,
    nheight: u32,
    filter: FilterType
) -> ImageBuffer<I::Pixel, Vec<<I::Pixel as Pixel>::Subpixel>>
where
    I::Pixel: 'static,
    <I::Pixel as Pixel>::Subpixel: 'static,
```

The image parameter takes an image that implements the GenericImageView trait. So we know we need to receive some kind of image data that can be transformed into a type that implements GenericImageView. The return type is an ImageBuffer, which can be transformed into something that JavaScript can interpret as an image. It also takes the new width (nwidth) and new height (nheight) as u32. The final parameter filter takes an enum called FilterType. This allows you

---

[13]Although we can avoid passing the width and height parameter and derive those values from the image itself, it's easier to pass them because the functions from the image crate need them.

[14]https://docs.rs/image/0.23.3/image/imageops/fn.resize.html

211

to select which algorithm to use to scale up the image. You can choose the Nearest Neighbor algorithm[15] for its simplicity and speed.

So now we know that we need something that can be transformed into something that implements the GenericImageView trait. Maybe we can also see what the frontend can provide. You can create a frontend project inside the current wasm-image-processing folder as before:

```
npm init wasm-app client
```

Inside the client/index.html file, copy and paste the following HTML code (Listing 6-9).

***Listing 6-9.*** HTML Page for the Image-Processing Frontend

```
<!DOCTYPE html>
<html>
  <head>
    <meta charset="utf-8">
    <title>Cat image processor</title>
  </head>
  <body>
    <noscript>
      This page contains WebAssembly and JavaScript content,
      please enable JavaScript in your browser.
    </noscript>
    <input type="file"
      name="image-upload"
      id="image-upload"
      value=""
    >
```

---

[15]https://en.wikipedia.org/wiki/Image_scaling#Nearest-neighbor_interpolation

```
<br>
<button id="shrink">Shrink</button>
<br>
<canvas id="preview"></canvas>

<script src="./bootstrap.js"></script>
  </body>
</html>
```

The page consists of the following elements:

- `<input type="file">`: This is the file selector that allows you to select an image from your computer.

- `<button>Shrink</button>`: When this button is clicked, you should call the Wasm function to shrink the image.

- `<canvas>`: This canvas is used the display the image.

The `<canvas>` is an HTML element that can be used to draw images with JavaScript. You can render an image onto it using JavaScript APIs. It also provides some APIs to read the rendered image data, which will be handy for converting an image into something Rust/Wasm can understand.

Let's break this process into three steps:

1. Use `<input type="file">` to load a local image onto the `<canvas>`.

2. Extract the image data from the `<canvas>` and pass it to Wasm for resizing.

3. Receive the resized image data from Wasm and display it onto the `<canvas>`.

# Loading an Image File Onto the <canvas>

You can load the image file onto the <canvas> just with JavaScript. Open the index.js[16] file and add the code in Listing 6-10.

*Listing 6-10.*   Loading the Image

```
function setup(event) {
  const fileInput = document.getElementById('image-upload')
  fileInput.addEventListener('change', function(event) {
    const file = event.target.files[0]
    const imageUrl = window.URL.createObjectURL(file)

    const image = new Image()
    image.src = imageUrl

    image.addEventListener('load', (loadEvent) => {
      const canvas = document.getElementById('preview')
      canvas.width = image.naturalWidth
      canvas.height = image.naturalHeight
      canvas.getContext('2d').drawImage(
        image,
        0,
        0,
        canvas.width,
        canvas.height
      )
    })
  })
}
```

---

[16]It is loaded in index.html through bootstrap.js, thanks to the template.

```
if (document.readState !== 'loading') {
  setup()
} else {
  window.addEventListener('DOMContentLoaded', setup);
}
```

This piece of code defines a `setup()` function. The function is called immediately if the page is loaded (`document.readyState !== 'loading'`); otherwise, it will be called once the `DOMContentLoaded` event fires.

In the `setup()` function, we monitor the `change` event on the `<input type="file">`. Whenever the user selects a new file with the `<input>`, the `change` will fire. The `<input type="file">` has an attribute called `files`, which returns a list of files you selected as JavaScript `File` objects. We can reach this `FileList` by referencing the `event.target` object (i.e., the `<input type="file">`).

To draw this file onto the `<canvas>`, you need to convert it to an `HTMLImageElement` (a JavaScript representation of an `<img>` element). When writing HTML, you set the `src` attribute on the `<img>` element to specify the URL of the image. But the file we just loaded is from a local file system. How can we get an URL for it? The `window.URL.createObjectURL()`[17] method is designed for this. It takes a `File` object as input and returns a temporary URL for it. The URL's lifetime is tied to the `document` in which it was created. Therefore, the following code turns the loaded image file into an `HTMLImageElement`:

```
const file = event.target.files[0]
const imageUrl = window.URL.createObjectURL(file)

const image = new Image()
image.src = imageUrl
```

---

[17]https://developer.mozilla.org/en-US/docs/Web/API/URL/createObjectURL

After you set the `src` attribute and the file is loaded, a `load` event will fire. In Listing 6-10, we listen for the `load` event and draw the image onto the canvas. Because we didn't specify the width and height of the `<canvas>` element in HTML, it has a default of 300×150 pixels. But the image might have a different size, so you can set the `canvas`'s `width` and `height` to the `naturalWidth` and `naturalHeight` of the `HTMLImageElement`. These two values represent the intrinsic size of the image.

Finally, you can draw the image onto the `<canvas>`. But you can't draw directly to the `HTMLCanvasElement` (i.e., the return value of `document.getElementById('preview')`). You'll need to first get the 2D drawing context by calling `canvas.getContext('2d')`. Only after that can you call the `.drawImage()` function on that context. The `drawImage()` function can take three arguments:

- `image`: The `HTMLImageElement` you created from the file.

- `dx`: The x-axis coordinate of the top-left corner of the image's position.

- `dy`: The y-axis coordinate of the top-left corner of the image's position.

Both `dx` and `dy` are set to 0 so the image's top-left corner matches the canvas's top-left corner.

To test this code, run `wasm-pack build` in the `wasm-image-processing` folder. This generates the Wasm module for the client to consume. Then run `npm install` followed by `npm run start` inside the `wasm-image-processing/client` directory. The preconfigured `webpack-dev-server` will start running. You can open a browser and visit `http://localhost:8080` to see the page in action (Figure 6-2).

# Passing the Image to Wasm

Now the images can be loaded onto the <canvas>, but what kind of data format can the canvas represent? As mentioned, images can be represented as a collection of pixels; each pixel's color can be represented by integers. Therefore, an integer array can be a good fit because both JavaScript and Rust can easily handle it.

As mentioned, a common way to represent an image is to store each pixel as four numbers:

- R: The intensity of the red channel

- G: The intensity of the green channel

- B: The intensity of the blue channel

- A: The Alpha channel, which indicates the transparency of the pixel. Alpha of 0% means totally transparent and Alpha of 100% means totally opaque.

If a u8 represents each value, then it can range between 0 and 255. On the Rust side, this can be represented by a Vec<u8>. On the JavaScript side, it can be represented by a Uint8ClampedArray[18]

On the Rust side, you can now complete the function definition, updating the lib.rs file as in Listing 6-11.

***Listing 6-11.*** Complete Definition of the shrink_by_half Function

```
extern crate web_sys;

mod utils;

use image::{RgbaImage};
use image::imageops;
```

---

[18]The term clamped in the name means the value is "clamped" to the range from 0 to 255. If you set a value larger than 255 it will become 255, and if you set a negative number it will become 0.

```rust
use wasm_bindgen::prelude::*;

// ... wee_alloc setup

#[wasm_bindgen]
pub fn shrink_by_half(
    original_image: Vec<u8>,
    width: u32,
    height: u32
) -> Vec<u8> {
    let image: RgbaImage =

        image::ImageBuffer::from_vec(
            width, height, original_image
        ).unwrap();
    let output_image = imageops::resize(
        &image,
        width / 2,
        height / 2,
        imageops::FilterType::Nearest
    );

    output_image.into_vec()
}
```

***Figure 6-2.*** *Loading a local image onto the* <canvas>

The original_image parameter is a 1D Vec<u8>. To reconstruct a 2D image from a 1D array, you need to also pass the width and height.[19] You can use the image::ImageBuffer::from_vec() function to turn the Vec<u8> back into an RgbaImage. Because the RgbaImage type implements the GenericImageView trait, you can pass this RgbaImage to imageops::resize to resize the image. Once you receive the resized image, it can then be turned back into a Vec<u8> with .into_vec() and returned to JavaScript.

On the frontend page, you can add an event listener to the Shrink button, so it triggers a call to the shrink_by_half() Wasm function. Set the index.js file as shown in Listing 6-12.

***Listing 6-12.*** Shrink Button Click Event Handler

```
import * as wasmImage from "wasm-image-processing"

function setup(event) {
  // ...
  //
  const shrinkButton = document.getElementById('shrink')
  shrinkButton.addEventListener('click', function(event) {
    const canvas = document.getElementById('preview')
    const canvasContext = canvas.getContext('2d')
    const imageBuffer = canvasContext.getImageData(
        0, 0, canvas.width, canvas.height
    ).data

    const outputBuffer = wasmImage.shrink_by_half(
        imageBuffer, canvas.width, canvas.height
    )
```

---

[19]In theory, you only need to pass either the width or the height, because the other one can be calculated from the size of the array and the specified dimension. But in this example, we pass both so the code is simpler.

```
      const u8OutputBuffer = new ImageData(
          new Uint8ClampedArray(outputBuffer), canvas.width / 2
      )

      canvasContext.clearRect(
          0, 0, canvas.width, canvas.height
      );
      canvas.width = canvas.width / 2
      canvas.height = canvas.height / 2
      canvasContext.putImageData(u8OutputBuffer, 0, 0)
  })
}

if (document.readState !== 'loading') {
  setup()
} else {
  window.addEventListener('DOMContentLoaded', setup);
}
```

Notice that we imported wasm-image-processing, which is the crate
in the top-level folder. When the button is clicked, you need to first get
the 2D context from the canvas. The context exposes a function called
getImageData, which can retrieve part of the canvas as an ImageData
object. The first two parameters specify the X and Y coordinates of the
top-right corner of the area you want to retrieve. The next two parameters
specify the width and height of that area. Here we get the whole
canvas. The ImageData has a read-only data attribute that contains the
Uint8ClampedArray representation of the RGBA values.

You can pass this Uint8ClampedArray to the wasmImage.shrink_by_half()
Wasm function imported at the beginning of the file. The return value will be
a Vec<u8> representation of the shrunken image. You can convert it back to
Uint8ClampedArray and wrap it in an ImageData.

To show this shrunken image on the `<canvas>`, you can follow these steps shown in the code:

1. Clear the canvas with `clearRect()`.

2. Set the canvas size to the new shrunken size.

3. Draw the new `ImageData` onto the `<canvas>` using `putImageData()`.

To test this application, follow these steps:

1. In the `wasm-image-processing` folder, run `wasm-pack build`. This compiles the Rust code into Wasm, located in the `pkg` folder.

2. Move into the `client` folder and run `npm install && npm run start`.

3. Open a browser and go to `http://localhost:8080` (Figure 6-2).

4. Click the Choose File button. A file selector window will pop up. Select an image file (PNG) from your computer (Figure 6-3).

5. Click the Shrink button (Figure 6-4).

---

**Note**    The method shown in this section is not the most efficient way. As a rule of thumb, you want to avoid unnecessary copying between JavaScript memory and the WebAssembly linear memory. Quoting from the official *Rust and WebAssembly* book[20]:

---

[20]`https://rustwasm.github.io/book/game-of-life/implementing.html`

*... a good JavaScript WebAssembly interface design is often one where large, long-lived data structures are implemented as Rust types that live in the WebAssembly linear memory and are exposed to JavaScript as opaque handles. JavaScript calls exported WebAssembly functions that take these opaque handles, transform their data, perform heavy computations, query the data, and ultimately return a small, copy-able result.*

Therefore, you might want to try loading the image directly in Rust/Wasm like this great open source project demonstrates: `https://www.imagproc.com/main`.

Another potential improvement is that we can offload the computation to a Web Worker. Currently, our JavaScript code calls the image-processing function on the main event loop. While the image-processing function is running, it might block further user interaction. Web Worker is a web technology that allows you to run scripts in the background thread so that it won't block the user interface. You can also find an example of a Web Worker in the `www.imageproc.com` code.

***Figure 6-3.*** *File selected*

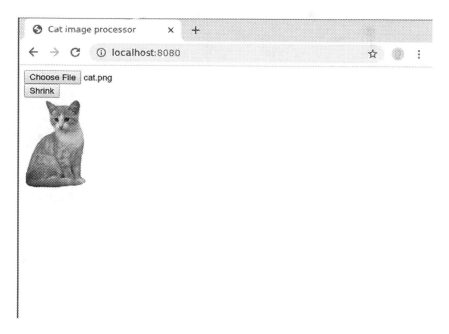

***Figure 6-4.*** *After clicking the Shrink button*

# Writing the Whole Frontend in Rust

Up until now, you've been building a web page in JavaScript and calling Wasm functions when needed. But is it possible to write everything in Rust? The answer is yes, but it relies on a programming pattern called the *Virtual DOM*.

The Virtual DOM is a concept popularized by the popular JavaScript framework React.[21] When you build a web page in plain JavaScript and need to change something on the screen, you need to call many DOM APIs *imperatively*. That means you need to say, "Get me this <p> element and change its text to foobar, then get that button and turn it red." But when the page grows more and more complicated, this approach might lead to chaos and human errors. Instead, React uses a *declarative* approach. You instead say, "I want this <p> to contain foobar, and I want the button to be red," and React needs to figure out how to get the page from the current state to your desired state.

Whenever the desired state changes, React will "render" the page to a Virtual DOM, which is an in-memory representation of the real DOM. The Virtual DOM can figure out which parts of the page changed compared to the previous state, and it can call the DOM API to update (or *reconcile* in React terminology) only the required part of the real DOM. This allows the developer to focus on the overall UI declaration instead of worrying about which part of the DOM to update.

If we build a Virtual DOM in Rust and compile it to Wasm, we can write the rest of the page in Rust, which interacts with the Virtual DOM. Then the Virtual DOM uses crates like web-sys to interact with the real DOM API to reconcile the difference. There have been many attempts. We'll introduce one of the most popular frameworks, called Yew.[22] Yew is heavily influenced by the design of React and Elm.[23]

---

[21]https://reactjs.org/docs/faq-internals.htmlwhat-is-the-virtual-dom
[22]https://yew.rs/docs/
[23]Another popular web framework/language for building frontend applications

# Setting Up Yew

First, let's set up a minimal project with Yew and take a look at a hello world project. Yew provides a project template just like wasm-pack, so we can easily set up the project. To start, run the following command to create a project using yew-wasm-pack-template.

```
cargo generate --git https://github.com/yewstack/yew-wasm-pack-template
```

When the command-line tool asks you for a project name, you can name it yew-image-processing.

---

**Note**   You might see an error message stating "Error replacing placeholders." This is a known issue with yew-wasm-pack-template, and it won't affect the functionality. It might be fixed in future versions. The project folder will still be created and you can safely continue.

Yew is very flexible with tooling. You can choose which Wasm build tool to use inside Yew. The options are:

- wasm-pack
- wasm-bindgen
- cargo-web

You can also choose which Rust-and-Web-API bindings crate you want to use:

- web-sys
- stdweb

In this chapter, we'll stick with the tools and crates maintained by the Rust/Wasm Working Group, which are wasm-pack and web-sys.

---

The project contains configurations for `wasm-pack` and `webpack`, which you are already familiar with from the `wasm-pack` template. The `README` documentation suggests using the Yarn package manager[24], which is an alternative to `npm`. These package managers accept the same `package.json` format, so you can still use `npm`.

The template also includes a TodoMVC[25] example. You can simply run the following command to start it:

```
npm install && npm run start:dev
```

A Webpack development server will start on port 8000. You can open a browser and go to `http://localhost:8000` to play with the example.

# A Hello World Example

The TodoMVC is too complicated as a hello world example. Let's simplify the example using the following steps:

1. Replace the content of `src/app.rs` with Listing 6-13.

2. Rename `todomvc.js` in `webpack.config.js` to `yew-image-processing.js`.

3. Rename `todomvc.wasm` in `webpack.config.js` to `yew-image-processing.wasm` (Listing 6-14).

4. Include `yew-image-processing.js` in `static/index.html` instead of `todomvc.js`.

5. Remove the TodoMVC CSS stylesheets in `static/index.html` (Listing 6-15).

---

[24]`https://yarnpkg.com/`

[25]TodoMVC is a project that implements the same to-do list application in multiple frontend frameworks. Its purpose is to help developers see how different frontend frameworks compare.

***Listing 6-13.*** New src/app.rs

```rust
use yew::prelude::*;

pub struct App {
    link: ComponentLink<Self>,
    value: i64,
}

pub enum Msg {
    AddOne,
}

impl Component for App {
    type Message = Msg;
    type Properties = ();
    fn create(
        _: Self::Properties,
        link: ComponentLink<Self>,
    ) -> Self {
        Self { link, value: 0 }
    }

    fn change(&mut self, _props: Self::Properties) ->
    ShouldRender {
        false
    }

    fn update(&mut self, msg: Self::Message) -> ShouldRender {
        match msg {
            Msg::AddOne => self.value += 1,
        }
        true
    }
```

```rust
    fn view(&self) -> Html {
        html! {
            <div>
                <button
                 onclick=self.link.callback(|_| Msg::AddOne)
                >
                    { "+1" }
                </button>
                <p>{ self.value }</p>
            </div>
        }
    }
}
```

***Listing 6-14.*** New webpack.config.js

```javascript
const path = require('path');
const WasmPackPlugin = require('@wasm-tool/wasm-pack-plugin');
const CopyWebpackPlugin = require('copy-webpack-plugin');

const distPath = path.resolve(__dirname, "dist");
module.exports = (env, argv) => {
  return {
    devServer: {
      contentBase: distPath,
      compress: argv.mode === 'production',
      port: 8000
    },
    entry: './bootstrap.js',
    output: {
      path: distPath,
      filename: "yew-image-processing.js",
      webassemblyModuleFilename: "yew-image-processing.wasm"
```

```
    },
    module: {
      rules: [
        {
          test: /\.s[ac]ss$/i,
          use: [
            'style-loader',
            'css-loader',
            'sass-loader',
          ],
        },
      ],
    },
    plugins: [
      new CopyWebpackPlugin([
        { from: './static', to: distPath }
      ]),
      new WasmPackPlugin({
        crateDirectory: ".",
        extraArgs: "--no-typescript",
      })
    ],
    watch: argv.mode !== 'production'
  };
};
```

**Listing 6-15.**  New index.html

```html
<!doctype html>
<html lang="en">
    <head>
        <meta charset="utf-8" />
```

```
    <title>Yew image processing</title>
    <!-- Stylesheets removed -->
  </head>
  <body>
    <!-- JS file renamed -->
    <script src="/yew-image-processing.js"></script>
  </body>
</html>
```
.

Now you can run npm install, followed by npm run start:dev, and refresh your browser to test it. You don't need to explicitly run wasm-pack build, because when you run npm run start:dev, the command triggers Webpack. In the Webpack configuration (Listing 6-14), there is a WasmPackPlugin configured so it will run wasm-pack build for you.

In a production build, Webpack will utilize wasm-pack to compile the src/app.rs file and other boilerplate Rust files to a Wasm module. It then will package other boilerplate JavaScript files into yew-image-processing.js. The index.html file then loads yew-image-processing.js, which then imports yew-image-processing.wasm and runs the Yew app.

To understand how this example works, you first need to understand the Elm architecture[26], which influences Yew. The Elm architecture consists of three core concepts:

- Model: The state of the application.

- View: A way to turn the state into the UI (HTML).

- Update: A way to update the state based on the message (Msg) triggered by user interaction on the UI.

---

[26]https://guide.elm-lang.org/architecture/

Their interactions are illustrated in Figure 6-5. Yew loosely follows this architecture.

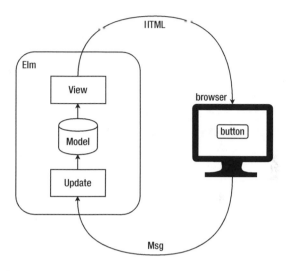

***Figure 6-5.*** *Elm architecture*

The hello world example has a counter as its Model. The counter is incremented whenever the user clicks a +1 button in the browser. The counter is also shown on the page, so the number updates whenever the Model changes (Figure 6-6).

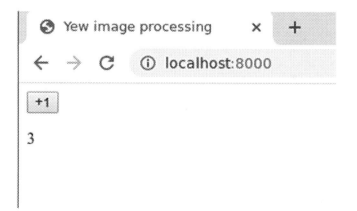

***Figure 6-6.*** *The Hello World Yew application*

The core of this example is in src/app.rs (Listing 6-13), which defines a component called App. But before we dive into its details, let's first understand how it's loaded in the page. In webpack.config.js (Listing 6-14), we see that the entry field is ./bootstrap.js. This means the entry point of this web page is the bootstrap.js file (Listing 6-16). The bootstrap.js file simply loads the compiled Wasm module (located in ./pkg) and calls the module.run_app() function.

***Listing 6-16.*** The bootstrap.js File

```
import("./pkg").then(module => {
  module.run_app();
});
```

.

The run_app() function is defined in src/lib.rs (Listing 6-17). The most important line in that function is

```
yew::start_app::<app::App>();
```

This line starts the Yew application by mounting the app::App component into the <body> of the HTML page.

***Listing 6-17.*** The lib.rs File Defines the run_app() Function

```
#![recursion_limit = "512"]

mod app;

use wasm_bindgen::prelude::*;

// When the wee_alloc feature is enabled, use wee_alloc as the
// global allocator.
#[cfg(feature = "wee_alloc")]
#[global_allocator]
static ALLOC: wee_alloc::WeeAlloc = wee_alloc::WeeAlloc::INIT;
```

```
// This is the entry point for the web app
#[wasm_bindgen]
pub fn run_app() -> Result<(), JsValue> {
    wasm_logger::init(wasm_logger::Config::default());
    yew::start_app::<app::App>();
    Ok(())
}
```

Finally, we can come back to `src/app.rs` (Listing 6-13). The file first declares a `struct` called App, which is the only component rendered to the screen. This `struct` contains a Model called `value`. This Model is the counter showing how many times the button is clicked.

We also implement the `Component` trait on App. The first function, called `create()`, takes care of the initialization of the component. As you can see, `value` is initialized as 0. The `view()` function is the key to turn the model into HTML. The `html!` macro allows you to write HTML syntax inside Rust, similar to JSX[27] in React. This `view()` function defines the HTML that will render a `<div>` containing a `<button>` and a `<p>`. Notice that the text inside the `<p>` is not hardcoded, but it refers to a variable `self.value`, wrapped inside a pair of curly brackets. This tells Yew to substitute the text with the value of `self.value` when `view()` is called. So whenever `value` changes, `view()` will be called, and the Virtual DOM will reconcile the change to the DOM and show it on screen.

How do you update the state? In Yew, you can update the state by sending messages to the component. In the same file, we defined a message `enum Msg`, which has only one variant called AddOne. The `update()` function on the App component handles incoming messages and updates the state accordingly. In this example, a `Msg::AddOne` message will increment the `self.value` model.

---

[27]https://reactjs.org/docs/glossary.html#jsx

To send the message when the button is clicked, you need to utilize the ComponentLink mechanism. ComponentLink is a way to register a callback that will send the message to the component's update method. As you can see, we added a link: ComponentLink<Self> field to the App struct. In the onclick event handler of button, we call self.link.callback(|_| Msg::AddOne).

# Reimplement the Image-Processing Frontend with Yew

You can also reimplement the client part of the wasm-image-processing project in Yew. The process is quite straightforward:

1. Create a Yew component.

2. Move the HTML page into the view() function of the component.

3. When the buttons are clicked, send Msg instead of calling JavaScript directly.

4. Convert the JavaScript button onclick handlers to Rust code using web-sys.

First, let's clean up src/app.rs to become a skeleton Yew component, then add the view() function to render the HTML, as shown in Listing 6-18.

***Listing 6-18.*** A Skeleton Yew Component That Renders the HTML Only

```
use image::imageops;
use image::RgbaImage;
use std::rc::Rc;
use wasm_bindgen::prelude::*;
use wasm_bindgen::{Clamped, JsCast};
```

```rust
use yew::services::reader::File;
use yew::{
    html, ChangeData, Component, ComponentLink, Html,
    ShouldRender,
};

pub struct App {
    link: ComponentLink<Self>,
}

pub enum Msg {
    // ...
}

impl Component for App {
    type Message = Msg;
    type Properties = ();
    fn create(
        _: Self::Properties,
        link: ComponentLink<Self>,
    ) -> Self {
        Self { link }
    }

    fn change(&mut self, _props: Self::Properties) -> ShouldRender {
        false
    }

    fn update(&mut self, msg: Self::Message) -> ShouldRender {
        // ...
    }

    fn view(&self) -> Html {
        html! {
            <div>
```

```
        <input type="file"
         name="image-upload"
         id="image-upload"
         value=""
         onchange={ /* ... */ }
        />
        <br />
        <button id="shrink" onclick={ /* ... */ }>
            { "Shrink" }
        </button>
        <br />
        <canvas id="preview"></canvas>
      </div>
    }
  }
}
```

In the App component's view() function, we use the html! macro
to render the HTML. The html! macro is similar to JSX in React, which
allows you to write HTML syntax in another language. However, the
html! is stricter in terms of syntax than most major browser's HTML
implementation, so you need to remember to properly close HTML tags as
XML tags (e.g., <br /> instead of just <br>).

Once the HTML is in place, you can start to migrate the JavaScript
code to Rust. Let's start with loading an image file onto the canvas. As in
the hello world example, you can attach a ComponentLink::callback()
to the <input type="file">'s onchange handler. The callback should
send a message to the update() function, which should then load the
image and show it on the canvas. The outline of this flow should look like
Listing 6-19. Notice that in the onchange handler, the event contains a
FileList object, and so we use js-sys to convert it into a Vec<File> for
ease of processing.

***Listing 6-19.*** Skeleton for Loading the Image Onto the Canvas with Yew

```rust
use image::imageops;
use image::RgbaImage;
use std::rc::Rc;
use wasm_bindgen::prelude::*;
use wasm_bindgen::{Clamped, JsCast};
use yew::services::reader::File;
use yew::{
    html, ChangeData, Component, ComponentLink, Html,
    ShouldRender,
};

pub struct App {
    link: ComponentLink<Self>,
}

pub enum Msg {
    LoadFile(Vec<File>),
    // ...
}

impl Component for App {
    type Message = Msg;
    type Properties = ();
    fn create(
        _: Self::Properties,
        link: ComponentLink<Self>,
    ) -> Self {
        Self { link }
    }
```

```rust
fn update(&mut self, msg: Self::Message) -> ShouldRender {
    match msg {
        Msg::LoadFile(files) => {
            // ... Load the file onto the canvas
        }
    }
    true
}

fn view(&self) -> Html {
    html! {
        <div>
            <input type="file"
             name="image-upload"
             id="image-upload"
             value=""
             onchange=self.link.callback(move |value| {
                let mut result = Vec::new();
                if let ChangeData::Files(files) = value {
                    let files = js_sys::try_iter(&files)
                        .unwrap()
                        .unwrap()
                        .into_iter()
                        .map(|v| File::from(v.unwrap()));
                    result.extend(files);
                }
                Msg::LoadFile(result)
            }) />
            <br />
            <button id="shrink" onclick={ /* ... */ }>
                { "Shrink" }
            </button>
        </div>
    }
}
```

```
            <br / >
            <canvas id="preview"></canvas>
        </div>
    }
  }
}
```

In the update() function, if we receive the Msg::LoadFile message, we need to do what lst:show-image does, but in Rust. You can convert all the JavaScript into Rust with the help of web-sys, which is a crate that defines the binding to Web APIs and Rust. The Rust code is shown in Listing 6-20.

***Listing 6-20.*** Loading the File Onto the Canvas

```
impl Component for App {
    // ...
    fn update(&mut self, msg: Self::Message) -> ShouldRender {
        match msg {
            Msg::LoadFile(files) => {
                let file = &files[0];
                let file_url =
                    web_sys::Url::create_object_url_with_blob(
                        &file,
                    )
                    .unwrap();
                let document = web_sys::window()
                    .unwrap()
                    .document()
                    .unwrap();
                let image = Rc::new(
                    document
                        .create_element("img")
                        .unwrap()
```

```
                    .dyn_into::<web_
                    sys::HtmlImageElement>()
                    .unwrap(),
            );
            image.set_src(&file_url);

            let image_clone = image.clone();

            let callback = Closure::wrap(Box::new(
                move || {
                    let canvas = document
                        .get_element_by_id("preview")
                        .unwrap();
                    let canvas: web_sys::HtmlCanvasElement =
                        canvas
                            .dyn_into::<
                                web_sys::HtmlCanvasElement
                            >()
                            .map_err(|_| ())
                            .unwrap();

                    let context = canvas
                        .get_context("2d")
                        .unwrap()
                        .unwrap()
                        .dyn_into::<
                            web_sys::CanvasRenderingContext2d
                        >()
                        .unwrap();
                    canvas.set_width(
                        image_clone.natural_width(),
                    );
                    canvas.set_height(
                        image_clone.natural_height(),
```

```
                    );
                    context
                        .draw_image_with_html_image_element(
                            &image_clone,
                            0.0,
                            0.0,
                        )
                        .unwrap();
                },
            )
            as Box<dyn Fn()>);
            image.set_onload(Some(
                callback.as_ref().unchecked_ref(),
            ));
            callback.forget();
        }
    }
    true
}
// ...
}
```

One important thing to point out is that the Image's onload handler takes a JavaScript function as a callback. To define that in Rust, you need to use a Closure. Because the image needs to be moved into the closure, yet we still need to reference it after defining the closure (when we call image.set_onload()), the image needs to be wrapped in an Rc so it can have shared ownership. Also, because the callback might be called after the update() finishes, we need to tell Rust not to drop the callback when it goes out of scope (i.e., when the update() function finishes). Therefore, we call callback.forget() at the end of the function.

Because web-sys contains a lot of Web APIs, web-sys puts each Web API behind feature flags. You should only enable features that you actually use, so you don't waste time compiling Web APIs you don't need. For this example, you need to add the following features to your Cargo.toml file (Listing 6-21).

***Listing 6-21.*** web-sys Features in Cargo.toml

```
[package]
// ...

[lib]
crate-type = ["cdylib", "rlib"]

[dependencies]
log = "0.4"
strum = "0.17"
strum_macros = "0.17"
serde = "1"
serde_derive = "1"
wasm-bindgen = "0.2.58"
wasm-logger = "0.2"
wee_alloc = { version = "0.4.4", optional = true }
yew = { version = "0.17", features = ["web_sys"] }
image = "0.23.10"
js-sys = "0.3.45"

[dev-dependencies]
wasm-bindgen-test = "0.3"

[dependencies.web-sys]
version = "0.3.4"
features = [
  'KeyboardEvent',
  'HtmlImageElement',
```

```
    'Element',
    'Document',
    'Element',
    'EventTarget',
    'HtmlCanvasElement',
    'HtmlElement',
    'MouseEvent',
    'Node',
    'Window',
    'CanvasRenderingContext2d',
    'ImageData',
]
```

Finally, you can convert the Shrink button code from JavaScript to Rust as well (Listing 6-22).

***Listing 6-22.*** The Shrink Button Callback in Rust

```rust
// ...

pub enum Msg {
    LoadFile(Vec<File>),
    Shrink,
}

impl Component for App {
    // ...

    fn update(&mut self, msg: Self::Message) -> ShouldRender {
        match msg {
            Msg::LoadFile(files) => {
                // ...
            }
```

```rust
Msg::Shrink => {
    let document = web_sys::window()
        .unwrap()
        .document()
        .unwrap();
    let canvas = document
        .get_element_by_id("preview")
        .unwrap();
    let canvas: web_sys::HtmlCanvasElement = canvas
        .dyn_into::<web_sys::HtmlCanvasElement>()
        .map_err(|_| ())
        .unwrap();

    let context = canvas
        .get_context("2d")
        .unwrap()
        .unwrap()
        .dyn_into::<
            web_sys::CanvasRenderingContext2d
        >()
        .unwrap();
    let width: u32 = canvas.width();
    let height: u32 = canvas.height();
    let image_buffer = context
        .get_image_data(
            0.0,
            0.0,
            width.into(),
            height.into(),
        )
        .unwrap()
        .data();
```

```rust
let image: RgbaImage =
    image::ImageBuffer::from_vec(
        width,
        height,
        image_buffer.to_vec(),
    )
    .unwrap();
let output_image = imageops::resize(
    &image,
    width / 2,
    height / 2,
    imageops::FilterType::Nearest,
);
let output_image_data = web_sys::ImageData
    new_with_u8_clamped_array(
        Clamped(&mut output_image.into_vec()),
        width / 2
    ).unwrap();
context.clear_rect(
    0.0,
    0.0,
    width.into(),
    height.into(),
);
canvas.set_width(width / 2);
canvas.set_height(height / 2);
context
    .put_image_data(
```

```rust
                        &output_image_data,
                        0.0,
                        0.0
                    )
                    .unwrap();
            }
        }
        true
    }

    fn view(&self) -> Html {
        html! {
            <div>
                <input type="file"
                  name="image-upload"
                  id="image-upload"
                  value=""
                  onchange=self.link.callback(move |value| {
                      let mut result = Vec::new();
                      if let ChangeData::Files(files) = value {
                          let files = js_sys::try_iter(&files)
                              .unwrap()
                              .unwrap()
                              .into_iter()
                              .map(|v| File::from(v.unwrap()));
                          result.extend(files);
                      }
                      Msg::LoadFile(result)
                  }) />
                <br />
                <button id="shrink"
```

```
            onclick=self.link.callback(move |_| {
                Msg::Shrink
            })
        >
            { "Shrink" }
        </button>
        <br / >
        <canvas id="preview"></canvas>
    </div>
    }
  }
}
```

Notice that you no longer need to export a Rust function to JavaScript. Everything is in Rust now, so once you've read the image data from the `<canvas>` and have done the proper conversion, you can directly call `image::imageops::resize()`.

# Other Alternatives

WebAssembly is a versatile platform for many applications, so there are many different tools and frameworks that focus on different topics.

The tools introduced in this chapter are mostly maintained by the Rust and WebAssembly Working Group.[28] That includes the `web-sys` and `js-sys` crates. But `web-sys` provides a very low-level API, which might not be user friendly. Their APIs are also a direct mapping to JavaScript APIs, so the syntax is not idiomatic Rust. There is an alternative implementation for Web APIs called `stdweb`.[29] It provides a higher-level binding between Rust and Web

---

[28]https://github.com/rustwasm/team
[29]https://github.com/koute/stdweb

APIs. It also uses a different build system called cargo-web[30], which doesn't rely on npm and web-pack like wasm-bindgen. Stdweb has wasm-bindgen compatibility since version 0.4.16. You can start using stdweb in wasm-bindgen-based projects, and it can be built using wasm-bindgen tooling.

There has also been effort from the Rust and WebAssembly Working Group to build a high-level toolkit, called gloo.[31] However, the toolkit development seems to be less active recently.

There are also many frontend frameworks similar to Yew. They are mostly inspired by popular frontend frameworks and patterns in other languages, like Elm, React, and Redux. Just to name a few (in alphabetical order):

- Darco[32]: Inspired by Elm and Redux.

- Percy[33]: Supports isomorphic web application, meaning the same code runs on the server side and on the client side.

- Rust-dominator[34]

- Seed[35]: Inspired by Elm, React, and Redux

- Smithy[36]

- Squark[37]

- Willow[38]: Inspired by Elm

---

[30]https://github.com/koute/cargo-web
[31]https://github.com/rustwasm/gloo
[32]https://github.com/utkarshkukreti/draco
[33]https://github.com/chinedufn/percy
[34]https://github.com/Pauan/rust-dominator
[35]https://seed-rs.org/
[36]https://github.com/rbalicki2/smithy
[37]https://github.com/rail44/squark
[38]https://github.com/sindreij/willow

But WebAssembly is not limited to the browser only. In theory, the Wasm runtime can be embedded (or can run standalone) almost everywhere. Some interesting examples include:

- Serve as backend web servers

- Power Istio[39] plugins

- Run on Internet of Things devices

- Drive robots

The Bytecode Alliance[40] is a cross-industry alliance that is driving the development of WebAssembly foundation outside of the browser. Its projects include:

- Wasmtime[41]: A Wasm runtime

- Cranelift[42]: A code generator that powers Wasmtime

- Lucet[43]: A Wasm compiler and runtime that allows you to execute untrusted Wasm code in a sandbox

- WAMR[44]: WebAssembly micro runtime

Many of these projects are built with Rust or work with Rust. If you are interested in the development of WebAssembly, you should keep a close eye on their development.

---

[39]Istio is a service mesh, which allows you to control, manage, and observe the network traffic between a network of microserivces.

[40]https://bytecodealliance.org/

[41]https://wasmtime.dev/

[42]https://github.com/bytecodealliance/wasmtime/tree/master/cranelift

[43]https://github.com/bytecodealliance/lucet/

[44]https://github.com/bytecodealliance/wasm-micro-runtime

# Index

## A

actix_web::Error helpers, 83, 84, 86

actix-web project, 57

actix_web::web::block() function, 33

add_cat_form() handler, 46–47

alert () function, 200

Amazon Web Service (AWS) account, 143, 144

api_config() function, 71, 91

API testing, 68–73

App::app_data() and App::data(), 36

.app_data() function, 26

as_pairs() function, 43

AWS Lambda, 6, 143–146, 159

## B

Built-in implementations, 85, 86, 88, 90

Bytecode Alliance, 249

## C

cargo-web, 225, 248

cat() handler, 49, 50

Catdex, 10, 16, 22, 23, 56, 144, 162

cat_endpoint handler, 78, 79

cats API, 64, 73–76

Certificate Authority (CA), 98, 101

client-rendered index.html, 70

CloudFormation, 162

Comet, 104

ConnectionManager's new() function, 35

crate-type, 199

Cross-origin resource sharing (CORS), 144, 187

## D

Database administrators (DBAs), 30

Developing Websites

actix-web, 52

adding cats, form, 38–47

async/await syntax, 9

cat detail page, 47–51

hello world, 11–15

ORM, 53

rendering dynamic template, 21–26

static files, 15, 16, 18–20

using database, 26–28, 30–35, 37

web domain, 9

Printed in the United States
By Bookmasters